# Rocky Mountain Wild Flowers

Managing editor
Norman Boudreau

Staff editor
Rigmore Adamson

Manuscript editor
Dorothy Burke

Designer
Gilles Robert et Associés inc.

Cover design
Gregory Gregory Limited

Colour separations
Prolith Inc., Montreal

Typesetting
Fast Typesetters of Canada Ltd., Montreal

Printing
D.W. Friesen & Sons Ltd.

the Athabasca and the Mackenzie Rivers, and to Hudson Bay via the North Saskatchewan River. The lower slopes of the valley are covered by a dense forest of alpine fir, but for several miles south of the chalet to Sunwapta Pass (6,675 ft) the flat valley bottom, though treeless because of the heavy accumulation of snow in winter, is covered by rich alpine meadows and low thickets of willow and ground birch.

From Sunwapta Pass the road descends steeply into the valley of the North Saskatchewan River. Near Mile 80, just beyond the entry of Nigel Creek from the east, the road cuts through a mature stand of Engelmann spruce. From the road there is a grand view of Cirrus Mountain and Mount Coleman, both well over 10,000 ft. Near Mile 90 the Alexandra River enters from the west. The road continues along the east bank of the North Saskatchewan River, which turns east at Mile 95 through a gap between Mount Wilson (10,631 ft) to the north and the almost 11,000-ft-high Mount Murchison to the south. On the dry slope near the approach to the bridge across the Saskatchewan River lies a small grove of low, twisted limber pine (*Pinus flexilis*).

The road then ascends the east side of the broadly U-shaped Mistaya Valley. Through openings in the forest one may catch glimpses of the area to the right of Waterfowl and Mistaya Lakes. Moose are often seen feeding on bottom vegetation of these shallow lakes. From Bow Pass (6,878 ft) and Bow Lake there is a splendid view of Crowfoot Glacier; the road then descends in long, winding curves into Bow Valley. Just north of Lake Louise the Banff Highway joins the Trans-Canada, which enters Yoho National Park in British Columbia through Kicking Horse Pass.

Opposite Mount Eisenhower, about 20 miles east of the Lake Louise cutoff, another branch-road leads south to Kootenay National Park in British Columbia. From this junction the Trans-Canada Highway continues east for another 20 miles to Banff, the only town and shopping centre of the park. The local administrative headquarters of the Rocky Mountain national parks are also located here.

From Banff, excursions can be made to a number of easily accessible points in Bow Valley. These should include a visit to the hot sulphur springs on the lower slope of Sulphur Mountain. From the Upper Hot Spring an easy trail leads to the summit of Sulphur Mountain (7,495 ft). An all-day excursion to Lake Louise is a "must" for visitors to Banff. From the parking lot near Chateau Lake Louise (5,680 ft) a foot-path leads to Lake Agnes (6,880 ft), nestling in a hanging valley between Mount Niblock (9,764 ft) and the slightly higher Mount White.

## Introduction

*Rocky Mountain Wild Flowers* has been designed primarily for the use of the visitor to Jasper, Banff and Waterton Lakes National Parks, Alberta, to help him to recognize and know a little better the commoner and more spectacular wild flowers within their boundaries, mainly in the alpine and subalpine zones; and, because a great many of the flowers described and illustrated are also common in the alpine country to the south and west of these parks, it will also be useful there. In the Alberta parks most of the species described or illustrated may be seen within easy walking distance of roads open to the public.

### Jasper—Banff Highway

One of the trips most popular for motorists to the national parks in Alberta is from the town of Jasper to Banff via the Jasper—Banff and Trans-Canada Highways, a distance of approximately 187 miles.

For the first 21 miles this road follows the west side of the Athabasca Valley, mostly through lodgepole pine forest growing on floodplains, boulder outwash slopes and rocky screes. About 8 miles south of Jasper the road crosses the Astoria River, and soon after, a small side-road takes off for the chalet at the foot of Mount Edith Cavell. In an all-day excursion to the chalet and environs the visitor will see some superb scenery and will have an opportunity to make the acquaintance of a great many alpine plants, as well as of several arctic ones that find their southern limit here. Such an excursion may be made from Jasper; if made from Banff, it would mean an overnight stop at Jasper. Continuing toward Banff the road crosses the Athabasca River at Mile 21, just below the Athabasca Falls. At Mile 27 it passes through black spruce forest, and a few miles further on through aspen forest.

From Mile 58 there is a grand view of the Sunwapta River flats, showing some fine examples of floodplain plant succession in which the earliest pioneer species are the broad-leaved fireweed (*Epilobium latifolium*, p. 286) and the yellow mountain avens (*Dryas Drummondii*, p. 232). From Mile 70 there is a splendid view across the Sunwapta River valley to Dome Glacier, flanked by Mount Kitchener and Stutfield Peak, both well over 11,000 ft. From the chalet, at Mile 65, one may see tongues of the Athabasca Glacier and of the Saskatchewan Glacier south of the divide between Jasper and Banff parks, flowing from the Columbia Icefield. This icefield, which is the largest continuous icefield in the southern Canadian Cordillera, straddles the Continental Divide. Waters from the icefield flow to the Pacific Ocean through a tributary to the Columbia River, to the Arctic Ocean through

# Rocky Mountain Wild Flowers

A. E. Porsild
Illustrations by Dagny Tande Lid

National Museum of Natural Sciences
National Museums of Canada

©National Museums of Canada 1979

Published by the
National Museum of Natural Sciences
National Museums of Canada
Ottawa, Canada K1A 0M8

Catalogue No. NM95–17/2

Printed in Canada

ISBN 0–660–00073–3

First published in 1974 as Natural History
Series, No. 2, in cooperation with Parks
Canada, Department of Indian and
Northern Affairs.
Reprinted 1979 and 1986

**Édition française**
*Plantes sauvages des montagnes Rocheuses*
ISBN 0–660–00069–5

 National Museums   Musées nationaux
of Canada          du Canada

National Museum    Musée national des
of Natural Sciences   sciences naturelles

# Table of Contents

Along the 3-mile path, one passes through four well-defined altitudinal zones of vegetation : the first, where Engelmann spruce forest is to be found, with its characteristic understorey of dwarf shrubs, arnicas and pyrolas ; the second, where alpine fir begins to replace the spruce, halfway to Mirror Lake ; the third, where alpine fir and Lyall's larch at Mirror Lake (6,655 ft) are the dominating trees, with an understorey of alpine heath mixed with a colourful assortment of alpine herbs ; and finally, the fourth, where scrub fir on the rock screes as well as moraines with patches of rich alpine herbmats on slopes below south-facing cliffs mark the timberline. A good many of the species illustrated in this book may be seen here, among them several truly arctic species on screes and cliffs at 7,200 ft at the head of the cirque beyond the west end of Lake Agnes.

Hoary marmots and the smaller pikas are common in the rockslides above timberline ; along the trail through the forest the mantled ground-squirrel, locally known as "big chipmunk", is common, and becomes very bold, loudly demanding a toll of peanuts from every passerby ; white-tailed ptarmigan are often observed in the cirque, and mountain goats may be seen on rocky ledges far above, while eagles circle overhead.

## How to use this book

The plants described and illustrated are grouped in the conventional manner of floristic manuals, beginning with the most primitive, such as the ferns and fern-allies lacking true flowers and reproducing by spores. Within this framework, the plants are grouped first within the plant family to which they belong and, further, within their proper genus. Thus, an anemone will be found in the Buttercup Family (Ranunculaceae) under the genus *Anemone*. Within each family the genera are alphabetically arranged. A brief description is provided for all the larger families dealt with ; for most of these, the genera represented within the area are enumerated, and the approximate number of species known for the area is given.

Common names are recorded where available, but because relatively few wild flowers have universally recognized common names, their Latin (or technical) names, internationally recognized and understood by botanists throughout the world, are always used, so that technical manuals may be consulted for confirmation or for further details. For this purpose, the most useful manual, and the only one dealing entirely with the flora of the province, is *Flora of Alberta* by the late Professor

3

E. H. Moss of the University of Alberta, published in 1959. This volume contains excellent keys and descriptions and, as stated in its introduction, is "a pioneer effort to record and describe vascular plants of Alberta", including a good many then known to grow in the mountains. Unfortunately *Flora of Alberta* has no illustrations, so that the user who has little or no practical experience with the plants may find it difficult to visualize what the plant described actually looks like.

Of some 1,250 plants known to the writer from the national parks of Alberta, about 250 of the more easily recognized and showy flowers are illustrated in colour in this book. Each illustration is accompanied by non-technical notes on size and general habit of the plant, and on where to look for it. Supplementary notes and descriptions are provided for some 180 similar or related species, for which separate illustrations could not be provided.

Throughout the text, measurements of plants and parts of plants are given in the metric system, now universally adopted in scientific writing. For the convenience of readers not familiar with the system, a conversion scale is printed inside the back cover.

For most of the species described and illustrated, some general observations have been added about their distribution in the Rocky Mountains and elsewhere. Thus, some of the plants occurring in the Alberta Rocky Mountain parks are said to be "Cordilleran", which, taken in a broad sense, means they are peculiar or endemic to the Rocky Mountain area ; but, for those dealt with here, it means they are peculiar largely to the middle and northern parts of the area. Incidentally the range of some members of the Cordilleran group extends north into the mountains of the Yukon and Alaska, but does not cross into eastern Asia. "Circumpolar" or "circumboreal" plants are wide-ranging species, distributed more or less continuously across arctic-alpine or subarctic North America, northern Europe and northern Asia. Members of still another large group are designated as native or endemic to "North America" or "northwestern America". Finally, one group designated "amphi-Beringian" includes plants common to both northwestern America and eastern Asia.

It is well known that the plant cover of the earth, often referred to as "flora", varies greatly from place to place owing to differences in topography, soil and climate. The distributional patterns of plants referred to above are closely related to what happened during the last Ice Age, when an ice-sheet several thousands of feet thick, such as the one that even today covers seven-eighths of Greenland, formed, and eventually covered northeastern North America from Labrador west to the eastern flank of the Rocky Mountains, extending south beyond the Great Lakes. In Europe a great glacier formed in the mountains of Scandinavia, and from there advanced southward to the Alps and eastward across northern Russia into western Siberia; similar ice-sheets formed elsewhere in northern Asia. These ice masses destroyed all plant life in their advance, and along their southern fringes the climate became truly arctic. In North America an arctic flora survived the Ice Age in what is now northern United States. When the ice retreated, this arctic flora was replaced by plants moving in from the south. In unglaciated parts of the northern Rocky Mountains, the Yukon and Alaska, floras similar to those of today were able to survive the Ice Age.

When the ice-sheets began to melt, plants followed the receding ice-front and eventually reoccupied all the land once covered by ice. The present flora of eastern, central and most of northern Canada, therefore, is relatively young, having recolonized that vast area since the ice receded; in composition it is very different from the vastly older floras of the Rocky Mountains, the Yukon and Alaska.

In mountainous regions, a more-or-less-distinct altitudinal zonation of the plant cover can usually be observed. This zonation is due to the gradual lowering of temperature from the lowland to the summit of a mountain. Thus, in the Rocky Mountain parks, the lower parts of most mountains are densely wooded, whereas the upper parts may be treeless. In ascending a mountain, one finds that the trees decrease in size and become more stunted, but the upper limit of trees, or timberline, is generally quite distinct and is controlled by the summer temperature, which rather closely coincides with a mean temperature of 10° C (or 50° F) in the warmest month. On the warmer south side of a mountain, timberline is often several hundred feet higher than on the cooler and more shaded north side.

Precipitation also greatly affects the plant cover of mountains. Thus, the eastern foothills of the Rocky Mountains may be treeless and inhabited by drought-resistant prairie species. Precipitation usually increases with altitude; this explains why some of the richest and most lush assemblages of alpine wild flowers may be found above timberline, in sheltered alpine valleys where the plant cover is well protected by a deep blanket of snow in winter but in summer is abundantly supplied with water from melting snowbanks.

Finally, on exposed mountain ridges and peaks, vegetation is sparse and individual plants often cling precariously to rock crevices and ledges. Here a small assemblage of hardy species forms the truly alpine and arctic element of the mountain flora.

## Acknowledgements

I should like to thank my collaborator Dagny Tande Lid, of Oslo, Norway, who made the drawings for this book from living and specially-selected specimens, when she and her botanist-husband accompanied me for two months while I was engaged in a study of the alpine flora of the Alberta Rocky Mountains. Her great skill and knowledge of alpine and arctic plants are reflected in the excellence of her drawings ; they are the most valuable and useful part of this book. I am no less grateful to my friend the late Dr. Johannes Lid, for many years Curator of the National Herbarium, Oslo, whose collaboration in the field was invaluable.

A. E. Porsild
*Curator Emeritus,*
*National Herbarium of Canada*

15 November 1971

PTERIDOPHYTA
**Ferns and Fern-Allies**

Mostly green, fern- or rush-like plants without flowers, reproducing by spores.

Represented within the area by six families, of which the Fern Family (Polypodiaceae) with eleven genera and nineteen species is the largest. The remaining five families, each represented by one genus, are Adder's-Tongue Family (Ophioglossaceae) with five species of moonwort (*Botrychium*) ; Horsetail Family (Equisetaceae) with eight species of horsetail (*Equisetum*) ; Club-Moss Family (Lycopodiaceae) with seven species of club-moss (*Lycopodium*) ; Spikemoss Family (Selaginellaceae) with four species of *Selaginella* ; and Quillwort Family (Isoetaceae) with only two species of *Isoetes* (not included in text).

# POLYPODIACEAE
## Fern Family

Because few of the true ferns of the area thrive on soils rich in lime, they are comparatively rare; only a few species are common locally, and these only in places where soil, moisture, and exposure are suitable. Those found exclusively on calcareous rock or soil derived from it are rock-brake (*Cryptogramma Stelleri*); spleenwort (*Asplenium*); *Woodsia glabella*; cliff-brake (*Pellaea glabella*); and lip-fern (*Cheilanthes Feei*). The more common rock-brake (*Cryptogramma acrostichoides*), polypody (*Polypodium vulgare*), lady-fern (*Athyrium*), shield-fern (*Dryopteris*), Christmas- or holly-fern (*Polystichum*), bracken (*Pteridium aquilinum*), and several others prefer neutral or acidic soils; only the bladder-fern (*Cystopteris fragilis*) appears to be indifferent, although conditions to its liking are perhaps most often found on acidic rocks.

*Cheilanthes Feei* Moore
**Lip-Fern**
Fig. 1

A delicate, brittle fern, in habit resembling *Woodsia scopulina*. Rare and local on calcareous cliffs. Cordilleran.

Fig. 1 × 1/2 (× 3/1)

*Cryptogramma Stelleri* (Gmel.) Prantl
**Steller's Rock-Brake**
Fig. 2

A small, delicate cliff fern with dissimilar sterile and fertile fronds, the latter always taller than the sterile, its lobes narrow and entire, with inrolled margins covering the sori (fruit-dots). Not uncommon below timberline on moist calcareous cliffs, often by waterfalls or in moist crevices in shaded canyons.

*Cryptogramma acrostichoides* is a similar but densely tufted rock-brake and not so delicate as the preceding one. Blade of the sterile frond three-parted and its stalk straw-coloured and wiry; segments of the spore-bearing frond more numerous than in Steller's rock-brake (*Cryptogramma Stelleri*). Rather uncommon in rock crevices and screes on quartzite rocks.

Green spleenwort (*Asplenium viride*) is small, delicate, and tufted, with linear, 5-to-10-cm-tall, light green, once pinnate fronds, the pinnae roundish-ovate, lacking a stalk and merging into the deeply grooved, green leaf-axis. In habit it resembles *Woodsia glabella*, from which it is at once distinguished by its oblong spore-cases and non-jointed leaf-stalks. Circumpolar, alpine.

Bladder-fern (*Cystopteris montana*), with a creeping and much branched rootstock and a leaf-stalk twice as long as the triangular, three-parted blade, is much less common; it is alpine and should be looked for in damp places under alders.

Bracken (*Pteridium aquilinum*) is a tall, coarse fern, from an extensively creeping, deeply buried, black, hairy rootstock. The leaf-stalk is thick and wiry, sometimes 1 m high or more, and the blade is triangular, divided into two or three parts. Open woods in light, sandy soil; rare in Banff Park but common in Waterton Lakes Park. Circumpolar, nonarctic.

Fig. 2 × 5/4

*Dryopteris disjuncta* (Ledeb.) Morton
**Oak-Fern**
Fig. 3

Five species of shield-fern (*Dryopteris*) are known from the area studied. The oak-fern and the closely related and rather similar shield-fern (*Dryopteris Robertiana*) are 25 to 30 cm tall. Both are circumpolar and grow in rich, moist woodland soils, often on rocky wooded slopes, but may ascend above timberline. Two of the shield-ferns, *Dryopteris austriaca* and *D. Filix-mas*, are tall, tufted woodland ferns with green, feather-like fronds.

Two species of lady-fern, *Athyrium Filix-femina* and *A. alpestre*, have each been collected a few times within the range. They are a more or less circumpolar woodland species and look like some plumose species of shield-fern, from which they may be distinguished by having two cord-like vascular bundles in the leaf-stalk, instead of five as in *Dryopteris*. This is easily seen when the stalk is pulled apart and the bundles appear as separate strings.

Bladder-fern (*Cystopteris fragilis*) has delicate, herbaceous fronds 10 to 30 cm tall from a creeping, scaly, quite brittle rootstock ; the shiny, somewhat translucent stalk is brittle and much shorter than the linear-oblong, two- or three-parted blade. It is one of the commonest circumpolar ferns and should be looked for in moist rock crevices, often beside alpine brooks and in shaded areas.

Fig. 3 × 2/3

*Pellaea glabella* Mett.
**Cliff-Brake**
Fig. 4

Small and densely tufted, with a short, erect, scaly, brown-hairy
rootstock. Rare or occasional on dry, sunny limestone cliffs or among
broken rocks on screes. Cordilleran.

Fig. 4  × 1/1

*Polystichum Lonchitis* (L.) Roth
**Holly- or Christmas-Fern**
Fig. 5

Coarse fern with densely tufted, leathery, shiny, wintergreen, 25-to-40-cm-tall fronds from a stout, tough rootstock covered by old leaf-stalks, decaying fronds, and brown scales. Fairly common locally in herbmats and on moist subalpine rockslides, chiefly on quartzite rock. Circumboreal (with large gaps).

Polypody (*Polypodium vulgare*) has a rope-like, spongy, sweet-smelling and sweet-tasting rootstock covered with felt-like scales. Fronds wintergreen, 5 to 20 cm tall, pinnate with entire, yellowish green, smooth, leathery lobes; leaf-stalk jointed, directly on the rootstock. Damp moss on non-calcareous cliffs and slopes but here known only from Waterton Lakes Park.

*Woodsia scopulina* D. C. Eat.
**Cliff Woodsia**
Fig. 6

Fronds densely tufted from a thick, tough rootstock, blades sticky from minute stalked hairs, aromatic and very brittle when dry, 10 to 30 cm high. Cordilleran and rather common in Banff and Jasper Parks and through the eastern foothills, on warm and sunny slopes, in rock crevices, and on rock screes well below timberline, generally on non-calcareous rocks such as quartzite.

*Woodsia oregana*, with fresh green, smooth or sometimes glandular, oblong fronds, is also Cordilleran and rather similar, although it is much less common. Thus far, it has been collected only a few times within the area.

*Woodsia glabella* is totally smooth, with delicate, light-green, 3-to-15-cm-long, linear-lanceolate fronds; the jointed, smooth stalk of the frond just above the rootstock distinguishes it from the preceding species. Quite rare in the area, and always in moist, shaded crevices of calcareous rocks above timberline. Circumpolar, arctic.

Fig. 5   × 1/3   (× 1/1)

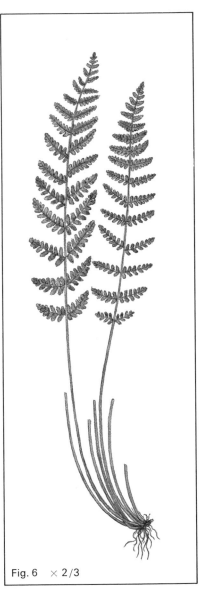

Fig. 6   × 2/3

# OPHIOGLOSSACEAE
## Adder's-Tongue Family

*Botrychium*

Smooth, erect perennials from a short, ascending rootstock and clustered, fleshy or fibrous roots. The stem simple, bearing a single variously divided, sterile blade, above which appears the fertile segment (sporophyll) of double rows of mostly sessile, globular, naked spore-sacs (sporangia).

*Botrychium boreale* (Fr.) Milde ssp. *obtusilobum* (Rupr.) Clausen
**Moonwort**
Fig. 7

Not uncommon in grassy herbmats above timberline, where it is often associated with *B. Lunaria*, in which the lobes of the sterile blade are kidney-shaped and of equal size. In the much rarer *B. lanceolatum* the sterile blade is three-parted and its lowermost lobes are lanceolate and acute. All three are low species with stems rarely over 15 cm high. *B. virginianum*, of rich lowland forest, has stems up to 5 dm tall; the sterile blade is thin, broadly triangular, and up to 15 cm long, and the spore-sacs are long-stalked.

Fig. 7   × 1/1

# EQUISETACEAE
## Horsetail Family

Perennial rush-like plants with creeping, freely branched, shiny
black rootstock ; stems annual or perennial, simple or branched,
jointed, hollow, and cylindrical ; the nodes solid, encased in a
toothed sheath ; branches, when present, whorled from the nodes.
Spore-bearing cone terminal. Eight species are known within the
range, four with annual stems and four in which the stems are
perennial and green the year around.

*Equisetum arvense* L.
## Field Horsetail
Fig. 8

Has two kinds of stem : one, which appears in spring and is pale
brown or whitish, with a terminal spore-bearing cone ; the other sterile,
green (see fig.), with whorls of branches at the nodes. Common
almost everywhere, from lowland to the upper limit of vegetation.

In *Equisetum pratense* and *E. sylvaticum*,
both woodland species, the fertile stem
when older produces whorls of green
branches. All circumpolar.

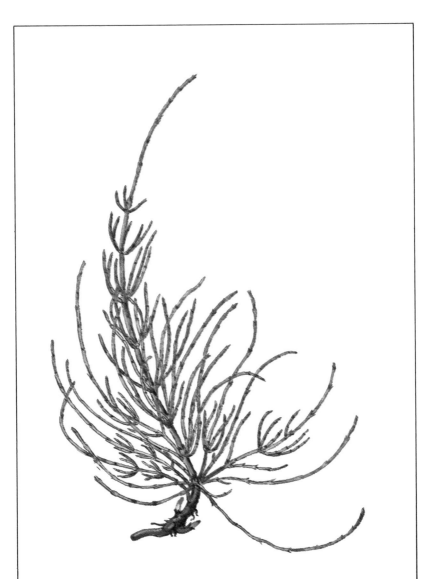

Fig. 8 × 1/1

*Equisetum palustre* L.
**Meadow Horsetail**
Fig. 9

Stems green and fertile, with whorled branches from the nodes. In the coarser and taller *Equisetum limosum,* some stems are simple and some are branched. Both are marsh plants forming colonies in shallow water by the edges of ponds or sluggish streams. Circumpolar.

*Equisetum variegatum* Schleich.
**Variegated Horsetail**
Fig. 10

Common in wet sand on lakeshores or riverbanks from lowland to the upper limit of vegetation.

Dwarf horsetail (*Equisetum scirpoides*) is smaller, the stems ascending or arched, mostly in small tufts from the slender rootstock. Often a dominant species in lodgepole pine forest but ascends to or slightly above timberline. Circumpolar, arctic-alpine.

Scouring rush (*Equisetum praealtum*) is a coarse plant with very rough stems 7 to 8 mm thick. Rare, and here known only from the vicinity of hot springs.

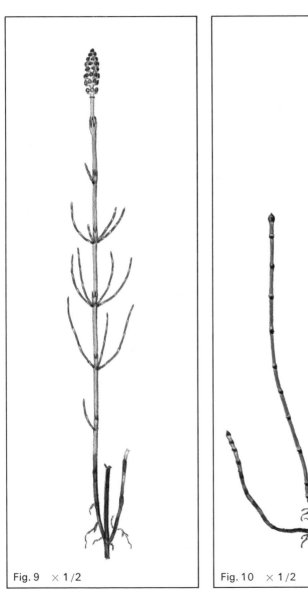

Fig. 9  × 1/2

Fig. 10  × 1/2

# LYCOPODIACEAE
## Club-Moss Family

Low, moss-like, evergreen, spore-bearing perennials with creeping
or tufted, freely branching stems, covered by rows of scale-like
leaves. Spore-cases usually terminal, cone- or spike-like, except in
*Lycopodium Selago* where they are axillary and kidney-shaped.

*Lycopodium alpinum* L.
## Alpine Club-Moss
Fig. 11

Stems pale, creeping, and freely rooting. Branches flattened, in
clusters ; spore-cases solitary and not stalked, at the tip of the
branches. Alpine herbmats and snowbeds. Circumpolar, low
arctic–alpine.

Ground cedar (*Lycopodium complana-tum*) is somewhat larger ; the stems
creeping just below the surface and the
2 to 4 spore-cases stalked. It is a heath
and forest species, rarely seen above
timberline. Circumboreal, sub-alpine.

*Lycopodium annotinum* has stems up
to 1 m long trailing above ground and
clusters of non-flattened branches with
spreading linear leaves. The spore-cases
solitary and not stalked

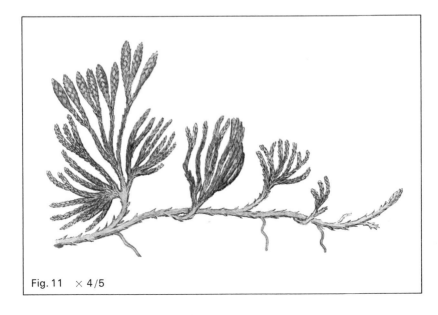

Fig. 11   × 4/5

*Lycopodium Selago* L.
Fig. 12

In small isolated tufts 5 to 20 cm high, with erect or ascending branches. The spore-cases in the leaf-axils. Common alpine in peaty soil. Circumpolar, arctic-alpine.

Ground pine (*Lycopodium obscurum* var. *dendroideum*) has aerial stems 1 to 3 dm high, erect and branched like a miniature pine tree, from a deeply buried, horizontally creeping stem. Spore-cases not stalked, at the tip of the branches. In open coniferous woods, very rare and only in Jasper Park. North America and eastern Asia; low arctic.

Fig. 12   × 5/4

## SELAGINELLACEAE
## Spikemoss Family

Small, perennial, moss-like plants with leafy branching stems.
Spore-cases in the axils of leafy bracts (strobiles) ; some containing
large spores, others small spores.

*Selaginella densa* Rydb.
## Evergreen Spikemoss
Fig. 13

Low, matted evergreen ; cone-like spore-cases sharply four-angled
on erect branches from a horizontally creeping and rooting green
stem. Common in dry sandy or stony places ; ascending to timberline.
Cordilleran.

*Selaginella selaginoides* (L.) Link
Fig. 14

Delicate yellowish green, matted or tufted ; rooted only at the base.
Spore-cases club-shaped, at the end of branches, the bracts and
leaves spreading. Damp calcareous places, in alpine situations, often
growing among or under larger plants or by brooks. Circumpolar,
alpine.

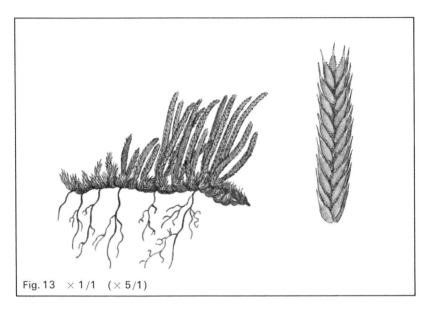

Fig. 13　× 1/1　(× 5/1)

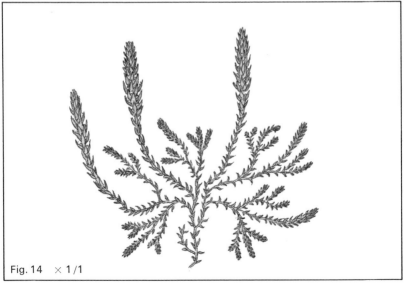

Fig. 14　× 1/1

## PINACEAE
## Pine Family

Trees or shrubs with needle- or scale-like evergreen leaves, or in
*Larix* deciduous leaves and mostly dry and scaly cones, but smooth,
blue, and berry-like in *Juniperus*.

*Abies lasiocarpa* (Hook.) Nutt.
## Alpine Fir
Fig. 15

Timberline species at once distinguished from the spruce by its
flat leaves, permanently erect cones, and smooth bark ; generally
found above the Engelmann's spruce and commonly on moist north
and west slopes. In sheltered places it may attain a height of 30 m or
more, but most often it is shorter, and near timberline it is commonly
reduced to low, sprawling, and almost impenetrable shrubbery,
resulting from rooting of the lowermost branches. In this manner a
circular live "hedge" is sometimes formed, in the centre of which the
dead remains of the parent tree can generally be seen. In early
summer, a refreshing, agreeable "brew" may be made by steeping the
young twigs in boiling water.

Fig. 15   × 1/2

*Juniperus communis* L. var. *saxatilis* Pall.
**Common Juniper**
Fig. 16

Low, depressed-ascending shrub with spreading needle-like leaves;
rarely more than 1 m high. Common on alpine slopes and in stony
places in the lowland. Circumpolar.

Fig. 16 × 3/4 (× 2/1)

*Juniperus horizontalis* Moench
**Creeping Juniper**
Fig. 17

Prostrate shrub with widely creeping and freely rooting branches.
Leaves of the mature branches scale-like. Common on dry rocky
slopes and ridges and on floodplains, and always on calcareous soil.
Ascends to about 6,000 ft in Banff Park. North America.

Rocky Mountain juniper (*Juniperus scopulorum*) is a small, bushy tree, here rarely more than 3 to 4 m high, and quite often a low bush. Rare and local in Banff, where, up to now, it has been noted only on dry south-facing slopes near Banff.

*Larix Lyallii* Parl.
**Lyall's Larch**
Fig. 18

Small- to medium-sized tree, rarely more than 10 m high, with a rapidly tapering, branchy, often gnarled and twisted trunk. It is the most alpine tree of the range and often forms pure stands near timberline.
It is of local occurrence everywhere and was found only in the southern parts of the area covered.

American larch (*Larix laricina*), though growing in subarctic and subalpine bogs, is a northern species, which barely enters the northeastern part of the range.

Western larch (*Larix occidentalis*) is a large, symmetrical tree with trunks up to 60 m high. In Canada mainly west of the Continental Divide.

Fig. 17 × 2/3

Fig. 18 × 2/3

*Picea Engelmanni* Parry
**Engelmann's Spruce**
Fig. 19

Large tree with trunk up to 60 m high and up to 2 m in diameter at breast-height, with a symmetrical, narrowly ovate crown. In general appearance it resembles white spruce (*Picea glauca*), from which it may be distinguished by its hairy branchlets and soft, light-brown cones, which have thin, flexible, rhombic-oblong scales. It often forms pure stands in subalpine valleys, where it commonly grows on the moister north slopes, ascending to 6,000 ft in Banff Park.

Two races of white spruce occur within the range. Both have smooth branchlets and firm, hard cones with stiff, reddish brown, rounded scales. Western white spruce (*Picea glauca* var. *albertiana*) is a medium-sized tree with rough, furrowed bark and narrow, spire-like crowns. It commonly grows in cold subalpine bogs and on gravelly or sandy floodplains or river terraces. Porsild's spruce (*Picea glauca* var. *Porsildii*) is taller, with a conical or narrowly ovate crown; the bark is smoother than in var. *albertiana*, and in young trees is densely covered with resinous blisters, as in balsam fir. It grows on soils such as rich alluvial floodplains and bottom lands.

Black spruce (*Picea mariana*) is smaller than white spruce; its cones are smaller and egg-shaped, and the twigs pubescent; it is mainly confined to boggy places.

Fig. 19  × 4/5

*Pinus contorta* Dougl. var. *latifolia* Engelm.
**Lodgepole Pine**
Fig. 20

The commonest forest-forming tree in the foothills and the drier parts of the range, where it commonly forms pure, uniformly aged stands; at once distinguished by having leaves in pairs. The small, 3-to-5-cm-long, hard cones with prickly-pointed scales remain un-opened on the trees for many years but open immediately in the heat from a forest fire. Some seeds generally survive a not too severe fire and germinate soon after, to start a new crop of trees.

Jack pine (*Pinus Banksiana*) is a small, scrubby tree commonly less than 30 ft high and usually growing in exposed places or on poor soil. As in lodgepole pine, the needles are in pairs and the cones are conical, 3 to 5 cm long, but directed upward whereas in lodgepole pine they are spreading.

Fig. 20   × 2/3

*Pinus flexilis* James
**Limber Pine**
Fig. 21

Leaves in clusters of five; cones light brown and up to 20 cm long, with leathery scales.

In the somewhat similar white-bark pine (*Pinus albicaulis* Engelm.) the cones are much shorter and remain closed for several years; the scales are thick and stiff. Both are small- to medium-sized trees, with short, thick, and often crooked trunks and branches, growing singly or in small clumps in open, wind-exposed places or near timberline.

Fig. 21 × 1/1

# POTAMOGETONACEAE
## Pondweed Family

Perennial aquatic plants, some wholly submersed, some with floating leaves and emergent spikes. Flowers small, bisexual, lacking sepals and petals, mostly in spikes or in axillary clusters. Fruit an ovoid, one-seeded drupe. Several species regularly propagate vegetatively, by axillary wintering buds or by rooting tubers. Pondweeds commonly grow in shallow ponds and lakes or in quiet streams. Several are important food plants for waterfowl, which, in turn, may distribute the seeds. Eight species of pondweeds are known from the Rocky Mountain parks, where they occur mainly in quiet lakes of the main valleys ; only two are known to reach timberline.

*Potamogeton alpinus* Balb. var. *tenuifolius* (Raf.) Ogden
Fig. 22

Rare or occasional in calcareous ponds.

*Potamogeton filiformis* Pers. var. *borealis* (Raf.) St. John
Fig. 23

Occasional to common in shallow ponds and lakes ; in Banff Park ascending to 7,500 ft.

Fig. 22   × 1/2

Fig. 23   × 1/2

# JUNCAGINACEAE
## Arrow-Grass Family

Smooth perennial bog or marsh plants with leafless stem and linear, somewhat fleshy basal leaves; flowers small and green, regular, three-parted, bisexual and in a terminal and spike-like inflorescence.

*Triglochin palustre* L.
## Slender Arrow-Grass
Fig. 24

Delicate plant from a short, erect, bulb-like rootstock, from which issue short, thread-like, bulb-bearing branches. Not uncommon in calcareous, boggy places, especially those fed by springs; mainly in the lowland.

*Triglochin maritimum* L. is much coarser, with scapes 30 to 40 cm high. Common in saline or alkaline marshes, mainly in the river valleys.

Fig. 24 × 2/3 (× 7/1)

# GRAMINEAE
## Grass Family

A large, economically important, but complex and taxonomically difficult family of annual and perennial plants with hollow, jointed stems known as culms, and narrow, parallel-veined alternate leaves, attached to the culm by their lower sheathing base. Flowers bisexual, one to several, in spikelets on a tiny axis called a rachilla; each flower with two scale-like bracts known as lemma and palet, which enclose the pistil and stamens, the latter usually three in number; each spikelet subtended by a pair of usually boat-shaped scales, known as glumes. The spikelets aggregated in open compound panicles, racemes, or cylindrical spikes. The largest single family in the Rocky Mountain parks, where it is represented by 140-odd species, distributed among 33 genera, of which *Poa* (bluegrass) with two dozen species is the largest.

*Agrostis humilis* Vasey
## Bent Grass
Fig. 25

Loosely tufted with slender, bright-green culms 10 to 15 cm tall, a narrow, somewhat interrupted panicle, and small, dark purple spikelets. Rather rare in damp, mossy places above timberline. Cordilleran.

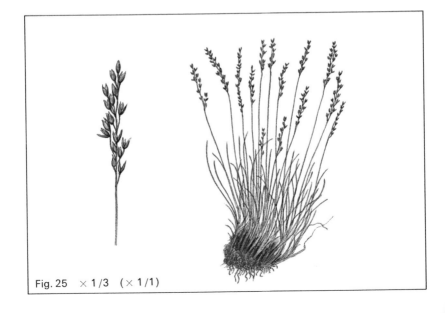

Fig. 25   × 1/3   (× 1/1)

*Bromus Pumpellianus* Scribn.
**Northern Brome Grass**
Fig. 26

Perennial. Culms up to 1 m tall, mostly solitary or a few together, from a tough, creeping rootstock; leaf-blades flat, smooth; panicle 10 to 20 cm long, the spikelets green, bronze, or purple-tinged, few- to 11-flowered; the lemmas with a straight awn; anthers 4 to 5 mm long. Common on floodplains and dry slopes, ascending to or slightly above timberline. Western America and eastern Asia.

Fringed brome grass (*Bromus ciliatus* L.) is similar but tufted, and the anthers are only 1 to 1.8 mm long. Subalpine meadows and snowslide slopes.

*Calamagrostis purpurascens* R. Br.
**Reed Bent Grass**
Fig. 27

Perennial, tufted, up to 50 cm tall, leafy, the leaves scabrous, inrolled; panicle dense and spike-like of one-flowered spikelets, each with a ring of soft hairs attached near the base of each flower; glumes scabrous, purplish; lemmas with a long, prominently bent awn protruding beyond the glumes. Common in well-drained, sunny places to or near timberline. North America.

The somewhat similar Cordilleran *Calamagrostis montanensis* Scribn. lacks runners and has somewhat shorter culms and an awn barely as long as the spikelet. In similar places but less common than *Calamagrostis purpurascens*.

The 1.5-m-tall blue joint grass, *Calamagrostis canadensis* (Michx.) Beauv., with its very leafy culms, from a creeping, slender rootstock, and a large, purplish green panicle, is common in meadows or open thickets. Its var. *Langsdorffii* (Link) lnm., which differs by its longer glumes and nodding panicle, is mainly alpine.

Fig. 26 × 2/3 (× 4/3)

Fig. 27 × 2/3 (× 3/1)

*Danthonia intermedia* Vasey
**Wild Oat-Grass**
Fig. 28

Tufted perennial, 3 to 5 dm high, with narrow leaves and few-flowered, open, spike-like panicles, 3 to 6 cm long, with five to ten spikelets; glumes pointed, 15 mm long, purple in youth, turning papery
white; the lemmas with a stout, twisted, bent awn. Common in alpine
meadows and on snowslides. North America.

*Elymus innovatus* Beal
**Wild Rye**
Fig. 29

Coarse perennial, with smooth culms up to 1 m high in small tufts
from creeping rootstock; leaf-blades firm, flat, or inrolled in drying.
Spike short and dense, 5 to 12 cm long; spikelets in pairs or solitary,
the glumes densely villous, the lemma with a short awn, the anthers
purple. Common locally and often turf-forming on well-drained
calcareous slopes or floodplains, ascending to timberline. Western
North America.

*Elymus glaucus* Buckl. is tufted and has
no creeping rootstock; the glumes and
lemmas are smooth; the awn is as long
as, or longer than, the body of the
lemma. Common locally in moist subalpine meadows. Cordilleran.

Fig. 28  × 1/2

Fig. 29  × 2/3  (× 3/1)

*Festuca saximontana* Rydb.
**Rocky Mountain Fescue**
Fig. 30

Densely tufted perennial; culms wiry and smooth, commonly less than 3 dm high; leaf-blades narrowly inrolled, pale blue-green, scabrous on margins; spikelets greenish or purplish at high elevations; anthers minute, 1 mm long or less. Common on rocky slopes to well above timberline. Cordilleran.

*Festuca altaica* Trin., with stout, smooth culms up to 9 dm high, forms small, firm tussocks; leaf-blades coarse, inrolled, 15 to 30 cm long; panicle lax and open, 10 to 20 cm long, drooping in age; the spikelets three- to five-flowered, 12 to 15 mm long. Alpine tundra, Jasper Park only, where it is very rare. North America and eastern Asia.

Fig. 30  × 1/2  (× 2/1)

*Hierochloë odorata* (L.) Wahlenb.
**Sweet Grass**
Fig. 31

Perennial from a creeping rootstock, with smooth culms 3 to 6 dm tall, and flat leaf-blades one-half to one-third as long. Panicle oblong-pyramidal, the spikelets three-flowered, shining, yellowish brown or purplish. Entire plant fragrant in drying. Occasional in damp meadows and by lakeshores. Circumpolar.

The arctic *Hierochloë alpina* (Sw.) Roem. & Schult. is densely tufted, with inrolled leaves and panicle shorter and denser; it has been collected once in Jasper Park. Circumpolar, arctic-alpine.

Fig. 31 $\times$ 2/3

*Koeleria cristata* (L.) Pers.
**Shining Spike-Grass**
Fig. 32

Densely tufted perennial with slender, smooth, erect-ascending culms up to 50 cm high; basal leaves short and narrow; the 4-to-5-cm-long, cylindrical, spike-like panicles composed of two- to four-flowered, compressed, shiny spikelets 4 to 5 mm long. Common in subalpine grassy places, chiefly on sandy soil, occasionally ascending to timberline.

*Phleum alpinum* L.
**Timothy**
Fig. 33

Perennial without runners; culm leafy, up to 6 dm high; panicle spike-like, ovoid or oblong, of one-flowered spikelet; the glumes prominently awned. Common by alpine brooks. Circumpolar.

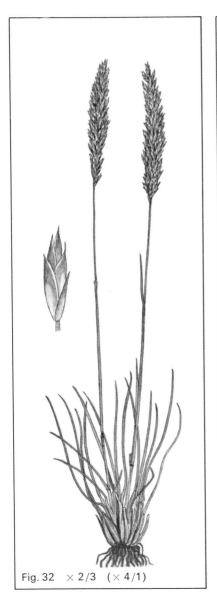

Fig. 32 × 2/3 (× 4/1)

Fig. 33 × 1/2

*Poa*
# Bluegrass

Low- to medium-sized, mostly perennial, tufted or stoloniferous grasses with two- to six-flowered spikelets in narrow or open panicles. Glumes keeled, one- to three-nerved; lemmas awnless, naked, or webbed at the base and along the median and lateral nerves, or with a tuft of cobwebby hairs at the base. A technically difficult and critical genus of which only a few species are readily recognized by the non-specialist.

*Poa alpina L.*
## Alpine Bluegrass
Fig. 34

Densely tufted, with stout, crowded bases covered by persistent white leaf-sheaths. Leaves mainly basal, short and flat, fresh green. Culms wiry, 15 to 30 cm high; panicle green or purplish, oval to broadly pyramidal. Common on moist alpine slopes.

Glaucous bluegrass (*Poa glauca*) is densely tufted; culms stiff, 15 to 25 cm high, slightly longer than the leaves. Culms and leaves glaucous (blue-grey) and scabrous; panicle narrowly lanceolate. A pioneering species in exposed rocky or gravelly places, where it often forms large tussocks.

Hairy bluegrass (*Poa lanata*) is loosely tufted from a creeping rhizome; culms 25 to 40 cm high, smooth; leaves one-third to one-half as long as the culms, 3 to 4 mm broad. Panicle pyramidal, open, the spikelets few-flowered; lemmas densely woolly. In sandy places on alpine slopes and screes.

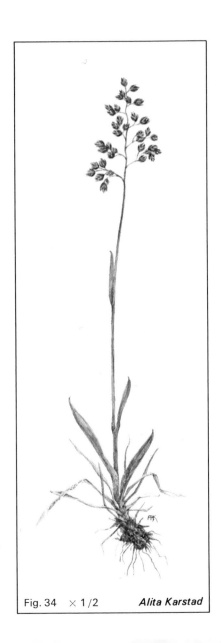

Fig. 34   × 1/2     *Alita Karstad*

# CYPERACEAE
## Sedge Family

Perennial grass- or rush-like plants with solid, three-angled, or cylindrical culms and narrow, linear leaves. Flowers perfect or unisexual,
arranged in spikelets; floral envelope sac-like, composed of bristles,
sometimes lacking them; stamens mostly three, their filaments slender;
stigmas two or three; fruit an achene.

Some 139 species, distributed among 5 genera, of which *Carex* is the
largest and taxonomically most difficult genus, richly represented in
the alpine zone. With its 120-odd species known from the Rocky
Mountain parks of Alberta, *Carex* is by far the largest single genus
represented.

KEY TO CYPERACEAE

a Flowers either male or female, in the same or in separate
  spikelets; stems three-angled

    b Achenes enclosed in a bottle-shaped sac (perigynium)    *Carex*, p. 60
    b Achenes enclosed in thin, tissue-like bract open at one
      side    *Kobresia*, p. 80

a Flowers mostly perfect, containing both stamens and
  pistils; the achenes with a ring of bristles at their base;
  culms round in cross-section

    c Bristles much elongated in fruit, silky    *Eriophorum*, p. 78
    c Bristles short, inconspicuous, or lacking

      d Base of style not enlarged, continuous with
        achene    *Scirpus*, p. 84
      d Base of style bulb-like, at the summit of the
        achene    *Eleocharis**

*Not described or illustrated

## *Carex atrosquama* Mack.
## Fig. 35

Tufted from short horizontal rootstock; culms slender, 3 to 4 dm tall,
longer than the soft, flat leaves; spikes three or four close together or
the lower stalked, commonly nodding, scales black; the perigynia first
green, turning golden yellow. Alpine meadows. Cordilleran.

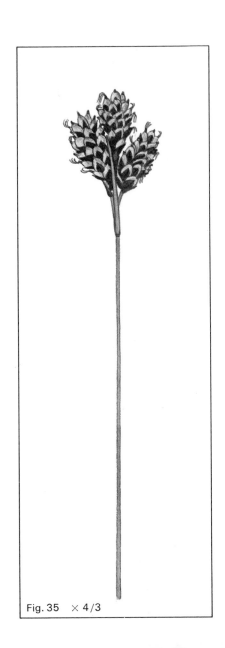

Fig. 35   × 4/3

*Carex concinna* R. Br.
Fig. 36

Loosely tufted from freely branching rootstock ; leaves flat, shorter than the slender, 5-to-15-cm-high culms. Male spikelet solitary and linear, the female two or three ; fruits hairy ; stigmas three. Rare and local in dry turfy places. North America ; arctic-alpine.

Fig. 36   × 1/1   (× 5/1)

*Carex festivella* Mack.
Fig. 37

Forming large, dense tussocks; culms stout, 3 to 6 dm tall, rough above and longer than the 3-to-4-mm-broad leaves. Spikelets five to eight in a dense, ovoid head. Alpine meadows. Cordilleran.

*Carex media* R. Br.
Fig. 38

Tufted with stiff, scabrous culms, much longer than the soft, flat, and scabrous leaves. Spikelets three or four in dense head subtended by a leafy bract; terminal spikelet club-shaped, male at base; stigmas three. Turfy places in dry alpine tundra. Circumpolar, arctic-alpine.

Fig. 37  × 4/3

Fig. 38  × 3/2

*Carex microglochin* Wahlenb.
Fig. 39

Loosely tufted dwarf species with short, slender runners and short, inrolled leaves, shorter than the 5-to-10-cm-tall, slender culms. Spike few-flowered, male at the summit; the 6-mm-long, straw-coloured fruits reflexed at maturity; stigmas three. Rare and local in springy places in calcareous fens. Circumpolar, low arctic—alpine.

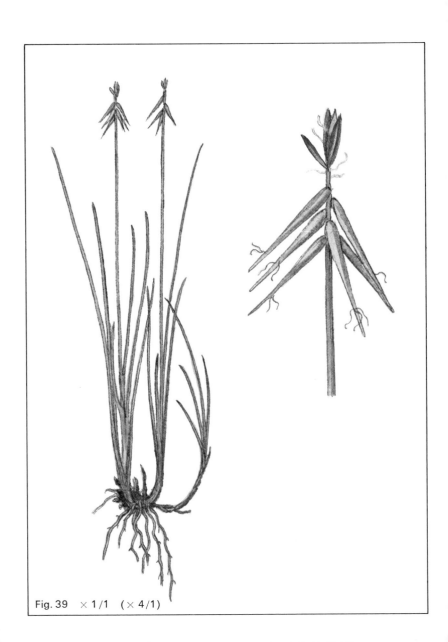

Fig. 39  × 1/1  ( × 4/1)

*Carex nardina* Fr. var. *Hepburnii* (Boott) Kük.
Fig. 40

Densely tufted, with persistent brown sheaths ; culms 10 to 20 cm
high, as long as, or slightly longer than, the narrow leaves. Spike
ovoid, male at the summit. Stigmas two. Calcareous, dry, grassy
or rocky slopes. Cordilleran, alpine.

Fig. 40   × 1/1   (× 4/1)

*Carex obtusata* Liljeb.
Fig. 41

Tufted, with slender, cord-like rootstock; culms slender, 8 to 12 cm long, longer than the narrow leaves; spike solitary, male at the summit; the fruits dark brown and shiny, stigmas three, rarely two. Calcareous, sandy fens. Circumpolar, arctic-alpine.

Fig. 41　× 5/4　(× 3/2)

*Carex petricosa* Dew.
Fig. 42

Culms mostly solitary, 15 to 25 cm tall, from bundles of slender, curly-tipped leaves, rising from an elongated, cord-like rootstock. Spikelets three to five, oblong, the uppermost male or sometimes female at the base, the lower all female; flowers 4 to 5 mm long; stigmas three or, rarely, two. Rare and local on stony calcareous slopes. Northwestern America; arctic-alpine.

*Carex Franklinii* Boott is similar but twice as tall, with larger, drooping spikelets. Very rare and local on calcareous riverbanks. Northwestern America; montane, low arctic.

*Carex praticola* Rydb.
Fig. 43

Tufted, culms 2 to 6 dm high, rough above, longer than the 1-to-2-mm-wide, flat leaves. Spikes three to six alternating and separate, bisexual; the male flowers at the base. Dry alpine heath. North America; subarctic-alpine.

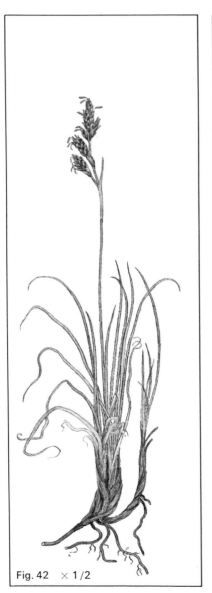

Fig. 42 × 1/2

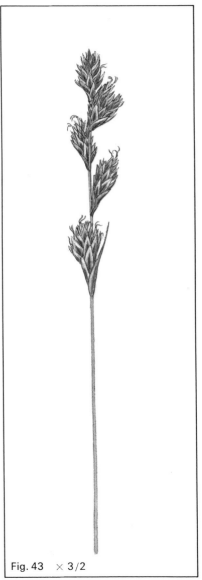

Fig. 43 × 3/2

*Carex pyrenaica* Wahlenb.
Fig. 44

Tufted, forming large, very compact tussocks; leaves narrow and inrolled, shorter than the 10-to-15-cm-tall culms; spike oblong, male at the summit, the fruits spreading or reflexed at maturity; stigmas three. Common or even dominant on moist alpine slopes where the snow remains late. Cordilleran, alpine.

Fig. 44 × 2/3 (× 2/1)

*Carex scirpoidea* Michx.
Fig. 45 ♂, ♀

Loosely tufted, with stout, horizontal-ascending rootstock; culms stiff, sharply triangular, 15 to 25 cm tall, and much longer than the broad, flat, scabrous leaves. Spikes solitary, those of male plant obovate, of female plant cylindrical; fruits hairy, stigmas three. Common in dry turfy places. North America; arctic-alpine.

Fig. 45   × 1/2

*Eriophorum Scheuchzeri* Hoppe
**Cotton Grass**
Fig. 46

Not tufted, culms mostly solitary, 10 to 30 cm high, soft and few-leaved near the base; spikelet solitary; when mature the soft, white bristles elongating to form a globose, fluffy head. In wet bogs or in water by the edge of shallow ponds, where it often forms pure stands. Circumpolar.

*Eriophorum callitrix* Cham. is similar but forms small, compact tufts with one or few culms 10 to 20 cm tall, its bristles pure white with a silky sheen. Rare, high arctic, alpine, growing in calcareous, turfy places.

*Eriophorum angustifolium* Honck. is not tufted and has flat, strongly keeled leaves and several drooping spikelets from the base of a leaf-like bract. In wet places, where it often forms pure stands. Arctic-circumpolar.

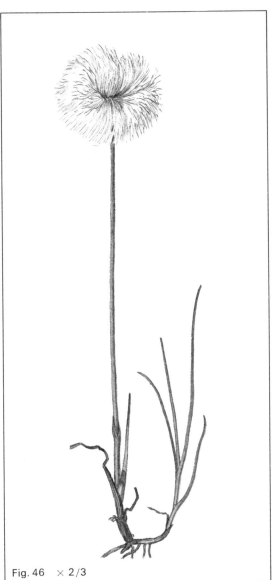

Fig. 46  × 2/3

*Kobresia myosuroides* (Vill.) Fiori & Paol.
Fig. 47

Densely tufted ; culms three-angled, slender, 10 to 40 cm high, from bunches of narrow, inrolled, curved leaves shorter than the culms ; inflorescence linear, 10 to 15 mm long. Common locally on calcareous sandy heath or windswept ridges.

Fig. 47   × 4/5   (× 3/1)

*Kobresia simpliciuscula* (Wahlenb.) Mack.
Fig. 48

Densely tufted ; culms three-angled, 10 to 30 cm high when mature, much longer than the leaves ; spike oblong-ovoid, composed of several spikelets. Common locally in moist calcareous and gravelly places. Circumpolar, arctic-alpine.

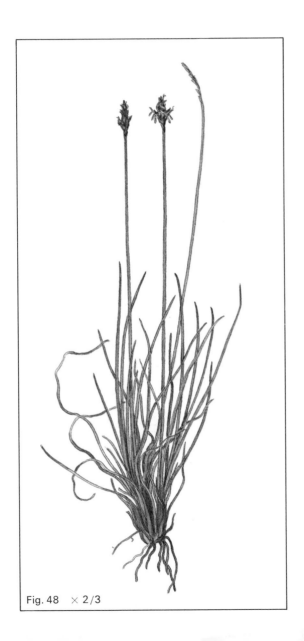

Fig. 48   × 2/3

*Scirpus caespitosus* L. ssp. *austriacus* (Pall.) Aschers. & Graebn.
Fig. 49

Low and very densely tufted, with smooth, wiry, erect-ascending culms, 10 to 15 cm high; culm-base firmly encased in persisting brown, scale-like sheaths, the uppermost with a minute blade; spikelet terminal. Forming firm, hemispherical tussocks in wet alpine tundra. Circumpolar.

*Scirpus hudsonianus* (Michx.) Fern.
Fig. 50

Culms scabrous, very slender, in small tufts from a horizontal or ascending rootstock; spikelet solitary, with a few soft, white bristles. Resembling a small cotton grass (*Eriophorum*) and by some authors placed in a separate genus, *Trichophorum*. Rare, in cold calcareous bogs. Circumpolar.

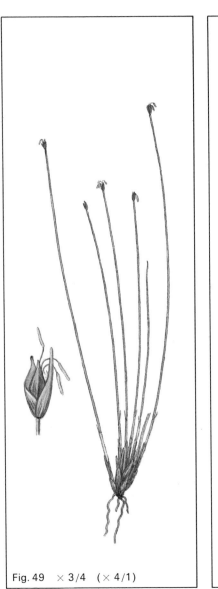

Fig. 49 × 3/4 (× 4/1)

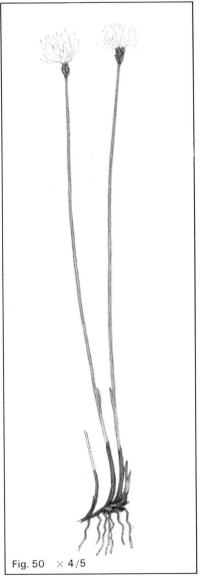

Fig. 50 × 4/5

# JUNCACEAE
## Rush Family

Herbaceous, grass-like herbs with small, inconspicuous, regular
flowers, consisting of three scale-like sepals and petals, three or six
stamens, single style with three stigmas. Fruit a three-valved capsule.

*Juncus albescens* (Lange) Fern.
Fig. 51

Small, compact tufts of slender, erect culms 5 to 20 cm tall, longer
than the smooth, narrow leaves. Inflorescence head-like of three
to five flowers subtended by a short bract. Calcareous fens (bogs)
or by edge of ponds. North America ; arctic-alpine.

*Juncus biglumis* L. is similar, but the
flowers are overtopped by a leafy bract.

*Juncus castaneus* Sm.
Fig. 52

Culms 1 to 5 dm tall, solitary or several together from a slender,
underground, stolon-like rhizome. Inflorescence usually of three
somewhat widely separated heads, each composed of several flowers.
In wet sand or clay by ponds or lakeshores. Circumpolar, arctic-alpine.

Fig. 51  × 1/1

Fig. 52  × 3/5  (× 3/1)

*Juncus Drummondii* E. Mey.
Fig. 53

Densely tufted ; stems 1 to 3 dm high, slender but wiry, from brown sheaths terminating in a bristle-like blade. Common on moist alpine slopes or ravines. Cordilleran.

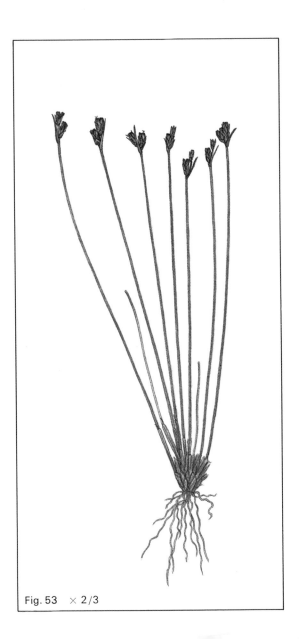

Fig. 53   × 2/3

*Juncus Mertensianus* Bong.
Fig. 54

Stems 1 to 3 dm high, leafy, from a horizontal rootstock. Heads solitary and globular, overtopped by a leafy bract 5 to 6 cm long. Moist alpine meadows or snowbeds. Cordilleran.

*Juncus ater* Rydb. has numerous approximate stems from a tough, scaly rootstock; flowers in small clusters below the summit, on the side of the stem. In wet sand or gravel by lakeshores. Cordilleran.

*Luzula parviflora* (Ehrh.) Desv.
**Small-flowered Wood Rush**
Fig. 55

Tufted from a stout, ascending rootstock; stems 3 to 7 dm high from cluster of mainly basal, flat leaves, 5 to 12 mm broad; inflorescence diffuse, flowers solitary or two or three together on slender branches. Subalpine herbmats, willow thickets, and woods. Circumpolar.

Fig. 54 × 2/3

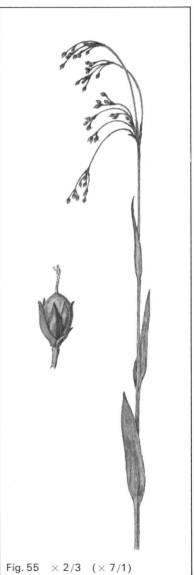

Fig. 55 × 2/3 (× 7/1)

*Luzula Piperi* (Cov.) M. E. Jones
Fig. 56

Similar to *L. parviflora* but lower, the leaves narrower, 2 to 4 mm broad, and the inflorescence of fewer but larger flowers. Alpine meadows and snowbeds. Cordilleran.

Fig. 56 × 2/3 (× 7/1)

## LILIACEAE
**Lily Family**

A large family of mostly herbaceous plants of very diverse structure and habit. Flowers three-parted and many quite showy, their calyx and corolla usually alike and mostly coloured; fruit a capsule or berry. Several are known to be poisonous. Represented here by 16 genera with a total of some 30 species, of which 10 are illustrated.

*Allium cernuum* Roth
**Wild Onion**
Fig. 57

Bulbiferous, smooth perennial with strong onion odour; leaves flat or channelled, fleshy, shorter than the erect flowering stem. Subalpine meadows. North America.

*Allium Schoenoprasum* L. is similar but taller; its leaves are round in cross-section and hollow, and the inflorescence is dense and capitate. The bulb and young stems are edible and taste like green onion. Subalpine boggy meadows.

*Camassia Quamash* (Pursh) Cov.
**Blue Quamas or Wild Hyacinth**
Fig. 58

Perennial, with up to 6-dm-tall, naked stem, from globose edible bulb, not unlike that of garden hyacinth; leaves all basal, 5 to 15 mm broad, linear, two-thirds as long as the flowering stem; fruit a dry capsule containing shiny, black seeds. Subalpine, damp prairie meadows; in Canada known only from southwestern Alberta and southern British Columbia. Recorded by early explorers as an important article of food among the western Indians.

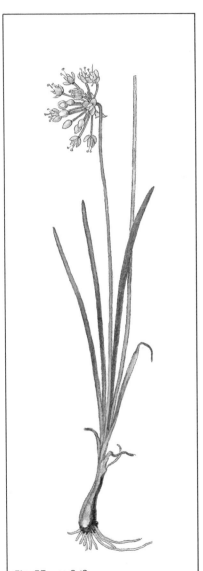

Fig. 57 × 2/3

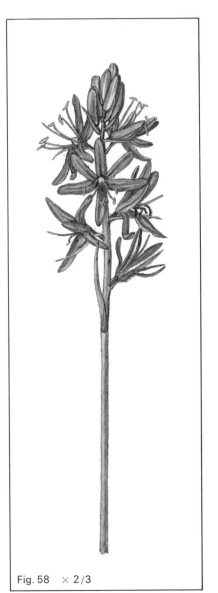

Fig. 58 × 2/3

*Clintonia uniflora* (Schult.) Kunth
**Bluebead Lily**
Fig. 59

Perennial from a creeping rootstock. Flowers one or two, bell-shaped, hairy, about 2 cm long, white ; fruit berry-like, blue, non-edible. Damp places in open subalpine woods. North America.

*Disporum oreganum* (S. Wats.) Miller
**Fairy-Bells**
Fig. 60

Perennial, with leafy, freely branching, 3-to-6-dm-tall, pubescent stems from a slender, branching rootstock ; leaves stalkless or nearly so. Flowers yellow, terminal, solitary, or few together in small clusters ; fruit dark red, non-edible. Damp places, often partly shaded. North America.

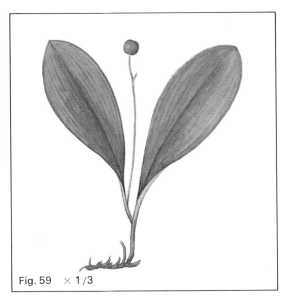

Fig. 59 × 1/3

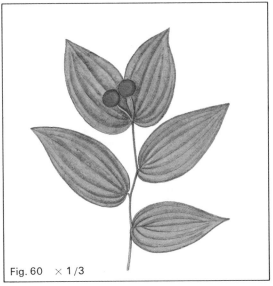

Fig. 60 × 1/3

*Erythronium grandiflorum* Pursh
**Glacier Lily**
Fig. 61

Smooth perennial from bulb-like base; flowering stem 2 to 4 dm tall,
one- to three-flowered, bearing a pair of oval-lanceolate leaves.
Common locally by alpine brooks and snowbeds. One of the showiest
mountain flowers in the area. North America.

*Lilium montanum* A. Nels.
**Western Wood Lily**
Fig. 62

Stem leafy, 3 to 6 dm tall from thick, scaly bulb; fruit a capsule,
2 to 4 cm long, containing numerous flat seeds. Rather moist
subalpine meadows. North America.

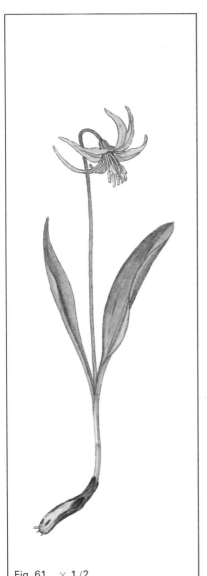

Fig. 61 × 1/2

Fig. 62 × 1/2

*Smilacina stellata* (L.) Desf.
**False Solomon's Seal**
Fig. 63

Perennial with a leafy, 1-to-4-dm-tall stem from an elongated root-stock; leaves stalkless, clasping, minutely hairy beneath. Flowers small, cream-coloured. Berry green with bright red stripes, turning black when ripe; not edible. In damp places, often among alders or willows. North America.

Fig. 63   × 2/3

*Tofieldia glutinosa* (Michx.) Pers.
**False Asphodel**
Fig. 64

Slender, tufted perennial from a short, ascending rootstock ; stems leafy, 2 to 3 dm high, sticky above ; leaves flat. Fruit a many-seeded capsule ; seeds tailed. Moist calcareous bogs. North America.

*Tofieldia pusilla* (Michx.) Pers. is smaller ; the stem is smooth, and the seeds lack tails. In alpine tundra. Circumpolar, arctic-alpine.

Fig. 64   × 2/3

*Xerophyllum tenax* (Pursh) Nutt.
**Bear Grass**
Fig. 65

Smooth, light green perennial with stems up to 1.5 m tall from
a thick rootstock; the lower leaves very numerous, long and tough,
linear, 2 to 4 mm broad, strongly one-nerved, with scabrous margins;
those of the stem needle-like and much shorter. The inflorescence
an elongated, many-flowered raceme, the lowermost flowers the
first to open. Fruit an ovoid capsule. Dry hillsides and dry subalpine
meadows, where it forms dense stands. In Alberta only in Waterton
Lakes Park.

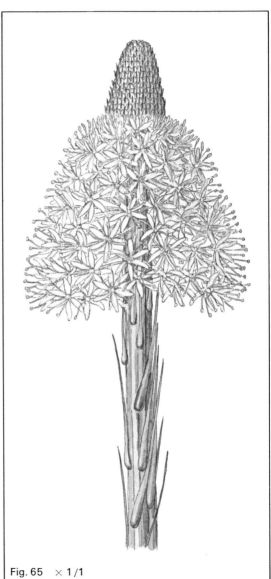

Fig. 65 × 1/1

*Zygadenus elegans* Pursh
**White Camas**
Fig. 66

Smooth bulbiferous perennial, 3 to 5 dm tall, with keeled, 5-to-10-mm-broad, somewhat fleshy leaves. Fruit a capsule containing numerous small, angled seeds. Flowers ill-smelling. Alpine tundra. North America.

False hellebore (*Veratrum Eschscholtzii*) is up to 2 m tall, with leafy stems and large, oval, entire, strongly veined leaves, from a thick, fleshy rootstock; flowers yellowish green, small and very numerous, in a very large, open panicle, the branches spreading or drooping; fruit an ovoid capsule containing numerous large seeds. Its great size and very beautiful foliage alone make it perhaps the most ornamental of western alpines. The roots, but also other parts of the plant, are deadly poisonous. Common locally in wet alpine meadows and by alpine brooks. North Cordilleran.

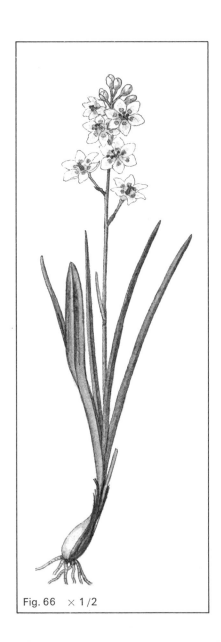

Fig. 66 × 1/2

## IRIDACEAE
## Iris Family

*Sisyrinchium angustifolium* Miller
**Blue-eyed Grass**
Fig. 67

Tufted, blue-green, grass-like herb from a short, ascending root-stock; leaves narrow and mainly basal; flowering stems wing-margined, simple or, rarely, branching; capsules globose, splitting at the summit. Damp subalpine meadows. North America.

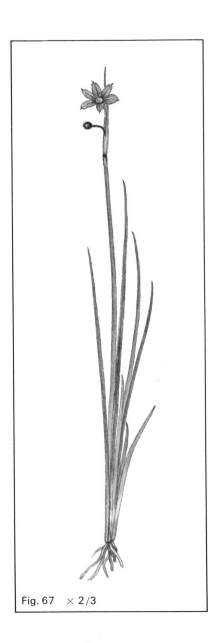

Fig. 67  × 2/3

## ORCHIDACEAE
## Orchid Family

Perennial herbs with tuberous, fibrous or scaly, coral-like rootstocks and entire leaves. Flowers irregular, three-parted, often showy; the sepals sometimes coloured, the lateral petals similar, and the middle one, called the lip, mostly dissimilar, and in some genera prolonged into a spur. Capsule three-valved, containing numerous minute seeds. A large, chiefly tropical family, represented here by 8 genera with a total of 21 species, of which 7 are in the genus *Habenaria*.

*Calypso bulbosa* (L.) Rchb.
## Venus's Slipper
Fig. 68

Although one of our smallest orchids, Venus's slipper is the most exquisite as well as the most elusive. Its favorite habitat is in pine woods where it grows in the damp litter of the forest floor, often associated with *Cornus canadensis* and *Equisetum pratense*. It flowers early in the summer, when the showy blossoms are much in evidence, only to vanish as if by magic when the solitary leaf- and flowering-stem shrivels and disintegrates, leaving only the fleshy corm shallowly buried in the forest floor. Nearly circumboreal, but not alpine, ascending only to the upper limit of lodgepole pine.

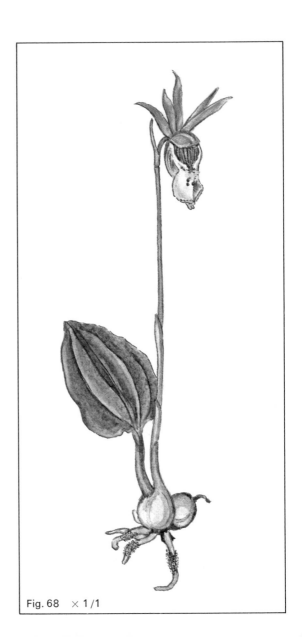

Fig. 68   × 1/1

*Corallorrhiza trifida* Chat.
**Northern Coral-Root**
Fig. 69

Small, pale-yellow or brownish plants, 10 to 20 cm tall, lacking proper green leaves, from a branched, coral-like rootstock. Flowers small, pale purple or green ; capsule egg-shaped, 8 to 10 mm long, pendent, turning purplish brown when mature. Common locally in mossy woods or in not too wet bogs or sometimes in the open *Dryas* mats. In Banff Park often above timberline. Circumpolar.

Two other species of coral-root are less common, both much taller and with larger flowers. Spotted coral-root (*Corallorrhiza maculata*) is often 3 to 4 dm tall, with a purple, leafless stem rising from a thick, tuber-like, non-branching rootstock. The lateral sepals three-nerved, and the lip 5 to 9 mm long and usually three-lobed, white with reddish spots.

In the equally tall striped coral-root (*Corallorrhiza striata*) the flowers are still larger, pink, yellow, or whitish, striped with reddish purple ; the sepals are one-nerved, and the lip is oblanceolate and not lobed.

All coral-roots lack proper roots and derive their food from decaying organic matter.

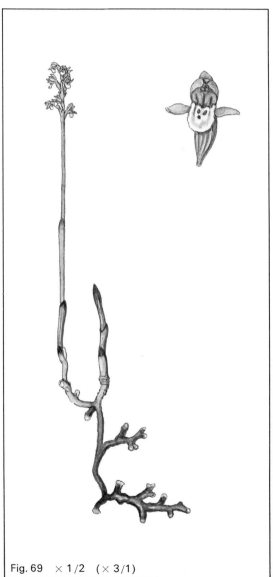

Fig. 69   × 1/2   (× 3/1)

*Cypripedium passerinum* Richards.
**Franklin's Lady's Slipper**
Fig. 70

Stems 15 to 25 cm high, leafy, from a thick, creeping, fibrous rootstock; the peduncle soft-hairy, bearing one or two flowers. Sepals green, the terminal sepal hood-shaped, the lateral one linear, longer than the lateral petals; the lip pale green, inflated and sac-like, longer than the sepals, about the size and shape of a sparrow's egg — hence the name *"passerinum"* meaning "of sparrows". Boreal North America.

The larger-flowered, fragrant, and much showier yellow lady's slipper, *Cypripedium calceolus* L. ssp. *parviflorum* (Salisb.) Hult., once common in the vicinity of Banff, has now been exterminated by excessive picking. It is still common locally in Jasper Park, in suitable places remote from flower pickers.

Fig. 70  × 2/3

*Habenaria hyperborea* (L.) R.Br.
**Northern Green Orchid**
Fig. 71

Stems solitary or a few together, stiff, commonly 15 to 25 cm, but occasionally 30 or even 40 cm high. The flowers yellowish green in an open, 5-to-15-cm-long spike, unscented or weakly perfumed. Common in rich herbmats, often by alpine brooks or occasionally in rich forests, ascending to or slightly above timberline.

Similar, but less common, is *Habenaria dilatata*, which differs from *H. hyperborea* by its slender and taller stems and its creamy white, strongly scented flowers. *Habenaria saccata* and *H. unalaschensis* may occur in the western part of the range; they have smaller flowers in long and very narrow spikes.

*Habenaria viridis* ssp. *bracteata* is low, with stems rarely more than 15 to 20 cm high, with short, ovate-lanceolate, shiny leaves, and with pale, yellowish green flowers supported by long, green bracts. It is common on dry grassy slopes and ascends to or slightly below timberline. North America.

Two species of rattlesnake plantain (*Goodyera*) have been reported from the range covered, where they should be looked for in shady and somewhat damp, mossy spruce woods. They have creeping rootstocks and fleshy, fibrous roots, and alternate and mostly basal leaves, often variegated green and white. The small, greenish white flowers appear in a spike. *Goodyera repens* var. *ophioides* is the smallest, with stems 10 to 20 cm high, and it differs from the taller *Goodyera decipiens* by its saccate lip with recurved margins, whereas in *G. decipiens* the lip is scarcely saccate and its margins are incurved.

Fig. 71 × 1/2 (× 3/1)

*Habenaria obtusata* (Pursh) Richards.
**Small Northern Bog-Orchid**
Fig. 72

Flowering stem naked and totally smooth, 15 to 25 cm high, with tuberous, fleshy roots and a solitary, stalkless, lanceolate-oblong leaf near the base of the stem. Flowers greenish white, in a few-flowered raceme. Common locally, mainly at low elevations, in partly wooded peat bogs or in moist willow thickets. Boreal North America; not alpine.

The flowers of the northern bog-orchid are regularly cross-pollinated by mosquitoes in a rather interesting manner. The mosquito enters the flower in search of honey, which the orchid produces and stores for this purpose in the slender, downward-projected spur at the rear. On leaving, the insect often carries on its head what looks like one or two tiny, yellow "horns". Under a lens these prove to be the club-shaped pollen masses, or pollinia, of the orchid flower. When the insect visits a second flower, the pollinia are unavoidably brought into contact with the orchid's stigma, causing a transfer of pollen and subsequent fertilization. A simple experiment in which the tip of a lead pencil is substituted for the head of the mosquito will demonstrate what happens. At the slightest touch the pollinia spring forward and attach themselves to the head or eyes of the mosquito by their sticky, discoid base; in this case, to the tip of the lead pencil.

Fig. 72 × 2/3 (× 5/2)

*Listera cordata* (L.) R. Br.
**Twayblade**
Fig. 73

Small and delicate, with stems rarely over 15 cm tall, and two stalkless, heart-shaped, opposite leaves, barely raised above the ground; the small, purplish brown flowers in a narrow raceme. Not uncommon, but easily overlooked in damp mossy woods or thickets. Ascending to timberline. Circumboreal.

*Listera borealis* Morong is taller; its pair of ovate-lanceolate leaves are well raised above the ground, the flowers yellowish green and larger, the prominent lip notched at the tip. Moist open woods, but not alpine. North America.

Fig. 73   × 4/3   (× 6/1)

*Orchis rotundifolia* Banks
**Round-leaved Orchid**
Fig. 74

Flowering stems solitary, 15 to 25 cm high, with a single round leaf near the base ; the roots thick and somewhat fleshy. The flowers 10 to 15 mm long, commonly three to six in an open raceme.

When closely examined, the fully expanded flower of the round-leaved orchid looks like some gay, dancing or flying elf-like creature. The lower lobes of the purple-spotted lip form the "body", the lateral lobes the "arms", above which a "head" is simulated by the two lateral petals and the upper sepal. The two pollinia form the closely set "eyes", and the pink or yellow stigma forms the "mouth", while the two lateral sepals perfectly resemble a pair of wings.

The round-leaved orchid is fairly common locally, in wet calcareous bogs watered from mineral springs, where it flowers from mid-July on. Boreal North America.

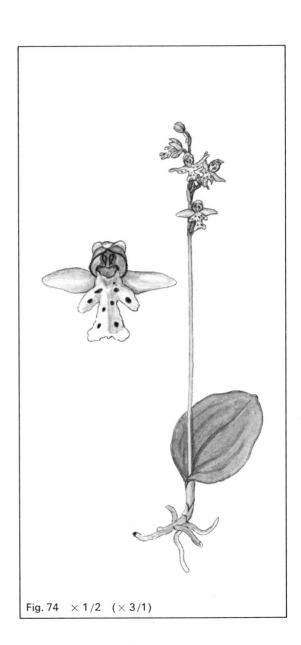

Fig. 74 × 1/2 (× 3/1)

*Spiranthes Romanzoffiana* Cham. & Schlecht.
**Hooded Lady's Tresses**
Fig. 75

One of the commonest orchids in the Rocky Mountain parks, where it is generally found in moist grassy places by the edge of calcareous bogs fed by mineral springs or, less commonly, in damp grassy herbmats by the edge of streams. Although reminiscent of the northern green orchid in stature and leaf-shape, it is at once distinguished by its small, whitish green flowers, arranged in a characteristically twisted spike, 6 to 8 cm long. The flowers are strongly vanilla-scented. North America.

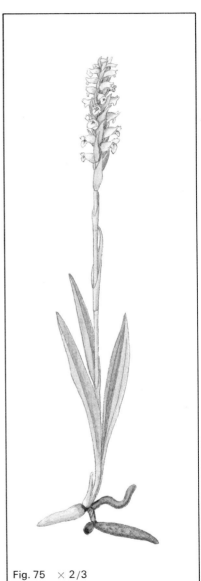

Fig. 75　× 2/3

## SALICACEAE
## Willow Family

Trees or shrubs with deciduous alternate leaves. The male and female flowers on separate shrubs or trees, solitary in elongated catkins. Fruit a capsule with numerous small seeds, each bearing a tuft of white, silky hairs. The family has only two genera: *Populus* and *Salix*.

Two species of poplar are native to the area. Balsam poplar (*Populus balsamifera* L.) becomes a large tree with reddish grey bark, and in age is deeply furrowed; leaf-blades ovate-lanceolate, dark green and shiny above, pale beneath on a round stalk. It is found mainly along streams; North America. Trembling Aspen (*Populus tremuloides* Michx.) has light green or white bark, somewhat furrowed in age, and rounded or somewhat heart-shaped, dull-green leaves on a flattened stalk. It grows on dry sandy slopes and flats, ascending to timberline; North America.

The genus *Salix* is represented in the area by about 35 species, of which 4 are tree-like or tall shrubs: *S. arbusculoides*, *S. Bebbiana*, *S. lasiocarpa*, and *S. lutea*, mainly restricted to riverbanks and lakeshores of low elevation; the rest are low shrubs, some erect-ascending, some creeping or even lying flat on the ground; most of them reach the alpine zone.

*Salix arctica* Pall.
## Arctic Willow
Fig. 76

Trailing and freely rooting; leaves 1 to 3 cm long, silky-pubescent in youth, becoming smooth; capsules hairy; scales black. Common on stony or turfy places from timberline to the upper limit of vegetation. Arctic-alpine, circumpolar. A very variable species; in the Rocky Mountains represented by a feebly distinct race, *Salix petrophila* Rydb.

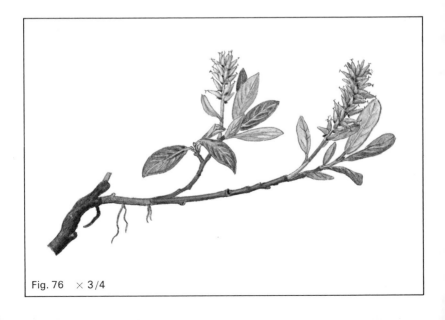

Fig. 76 × 3/4

*Salix Barrattiana* Hook.
**Barratt's Willow**
Fig. 77

Thicket-forming shrub with erect, much branched, gnarly stems, commonly less than 1 m high, growing most often in wet places by alpine brooks or in hollows where the snow remains late. The blue-green leaves hairy on both surfaces, and like the young twigs, somewhat sticky from a clear and colourless, oil-like substance, which penetrates the drying papers during pressing. The catkins appearing with the leaves and at maturity 6 to 10 cm long ; capsules hairy. Browsed by moose and elk. Cordilleran, from Alaska and the Yukon south to Alberta and British Columbia.

Fig. 77  × 3/4

*Salix glauca* L.
**Blue-green Willow**
Fig. 78

Erect-ascending shrub commonly up to 2 m high but in the alpine zone much lower. Young twigs commonly soft-hairy; leaves dark green above, paler and blue-green and hairy beneath. Bracts pale brown; capsules hairy. Common and often thicket-forming in well-watered sandy and gravelly places by riverbanks and lakeshores, mainly at lower elevations. Circumpolar.

Fig. 78   × 2/3

*Salix nivalis* Hook.
**Snow Willow**
Fig. 79

Prostrate, mat-forming dwarf species with tiny, oval-roundish leaves, often less than 0.5 cm long. Catkins at the end of leafy branches; few-flowered. Capsules reddish, grey-hairy. Endemic to the area; the smallest of the willows and perhaps the smallest woody species in the area; growing on moist alpine slopes and hollows where the snow remains late and where it is occasionally associated with the circumpolar net-veined willow (*Salix reticulata*), which is of similar habit but has 1-to-2-cm-long, net-veined, more or less leathery leaves.

*Salix vestita* Pursh var. *erecta* Anderss.
**Rock Willow**
Fig. 80

A very handsome, erect-ascending, up to 1.5-m-tall shrub with thick, oval, crenate-margined leaves, dark green above and permanently silvery-silky beneath. Bud scales bright reddish brown. Pistillate catkins 2 to 3 cm long at the end of leafy branches. Capsules greyish green, hairy. Calcareous, moist rock-crevices and screes. North America.

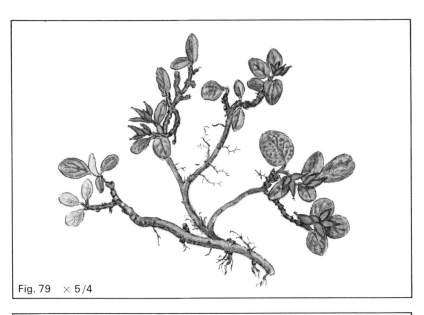

Fig. 79 × 5/4

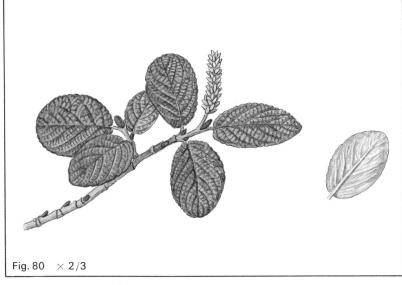

Fig. 80 × 2/3

# BETULACEAE
## Birch Family

*Betula occidentalis* Hook.
## White Birch
Fig. 81

Coppice-forming shrub 2 to 4 m tall, branching from the base, only occasionally isolated and tree-like, the bark reddish brown, shiny, never white, peeling as in paper birch. Never alpine, common mainly at low elevations in open forest or on river terraces. Cordilleran.

Ground birch (*Betula glandulosa* Michx.) is a depressed or ascending shrub with obovate to roundish leaves 0.5 to 3.0 cm long; its twigs and young branches are covered with resinous, wart-like glands; the catkins small and ovate. North America; low arctic, alpine. Here mainly above timberline.

Fig. 81 × 2/3

*Alnus crispa* Michx. ssp. *sinuata* (Regel) Hult.
**Mountain Alder**
Fig. 82

Thicket-forming shrub up to 3 m tall; in the mountains commonly with ascending stems owing to snow pressure, because it usually grows along creek beds or screes subject to snowslides. Above timberline, low and more or less depressed. Northwestern America.

River alder (*Alnus tenuifolia* Nutt.) is a lowland species; taller than the mountain alder, its leaves are dull green, not shiny, and its seeds are wingless. Cordilleran.

Fig. 82　× 3/5

## SANTALACEAE
## Sandalwood Family

*Geocaulon lividum* (Richards.) Fern.
**Bastard Toadflax**
Fig. 83

Leafy-stemmed, smooth perennial herb, 2 to 3 dm tall, from a slender rootstock; flowers small and green, lacking corolla. Fruit fleshy, bright red when ripe, edible but rather insipid. Damp places in open coniferous forest. North America.

Fig. 83   × 1/1

# LORANTHACEAE
## Mistletoe Family

*Arceuthobium americanum* Nutt.
**Pine Mistletoe**
Fig. 84

Small, fleshy, yellowish green plant, which is parasitic on the branches of conifers. Its branches are four-angled and its leaves opposite and scale-like; the small, inconspicuous flowers, male or female, appear in the axils of the scales. The fruit is a small, fleshy berry; when ripe the berry "explodes", ejecting the single seed, which may become attached by its sticky pulp to another branch of the host tree.

In the mountains the pine mistletoe is generally found on young lodgepole pine, where it forms broom-like clusters on the main trunk, usually well above the ground, or on the branches. Its occurrence appears to be periodic or recurrent and has the character of an infestation, which spreads and increases over a number of years until nearly all stands of young pine are infested. Because new growth of the lodgepole pine mainly occurs after a fire, the recurrence of the mistletoe infestation is probably similarly fire-controlled.

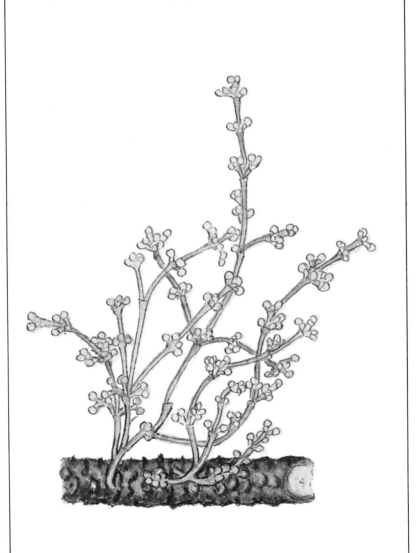

Fig. 84 × 3/2

POLYGONACEAE
**Buckwheat Family**

Alpine and mainly perennial herbs but in *Eriogonum* sometimes
with a somewhat woody base; leaves simple, mostly with membranaceous sheathing stipules above the swollen joints of the stem;
flowers mostly small but often numerous, in spikes, panicles, or
umbels; petals lacking; sepals separate or three- to six-parted,
sometimes petal-like; fruits tiny, dry nutlets.

In the mountains a small family of 5 genera with a total of 27 species,
of which nearly half are *Polygonum*, but very few are alpine.

*Eriogonum ovalifolium* Nutt.
**Oval-leaved Umbrella Plant**
Fig. 85

Similar to *Eriogonum subalpinum* (see Fig. 86) but smaller, the leaves
and scapes densely white-tomentose; flowers mostly pink, less often
white. Alpine, rocky slopes. Cordilleran.

Fig. 85  × 3/2

*Eriogonum subalpinum* Greene
**Umbrella Plant**
Fig. 86

Perennial with a somewhat woody base, from which radiate prostrate rooting branches. Leaves spatulate, smooth above, in basal rosettes. Inflorescence of small clustered flowers; petals none, the calyx six-parted, creamy yellow, turning pink in age and enveloping the nutlets. Alpine tundra and rocky ledges. Cordilleran.

Fig. 86   × 2/3

## *Oxyria digyna* (L.) Hill
## Mountain Sorrel
Fig. 87

Perennial herb, with a short rootstock bearing clusters of long-stalked, kidney-shaped, fresh green, somewhat succulent leaves. Stems naked or few-leaved, 10 to 30 cm high, bearing small reddish or green flowers. The succulent acid leaves and young stems are edible and excellent for quenching thirst. The mountain sorrel is one of the most wide-ranging circumpolar, arctic-alpine plants; common in moist places with good snow-cover in winter, throughout the Arctic and in most high mountain regions of North America and Eurasia.

*Koenigia islandica* L. is a tiny annual, often only a few cm high, with smooth, usually reddish, simple or branching stems bearing a few oblong-rounded leaves, those near the end of the stem usually whorled around the tiny, three-parted, greenish flowers. Very rare in the Canadian Rockies, where it is known only from a single station in Jasper Park. Circumpolar, low arctic.

Fig. 87   × 4/5

*Polygonum bistortoides* Pursh
**Bistort**
Fig. 88

Similar to the commoner *P. viviparum*, but stems taller and spike shorter, about 2 cm thick; bulbils lacking, flowers fertile. Moist alpine tundra. Cordilleran.

*Polygonum viviparum* L.
**Knotweed**
Fig. 89

Perennial herb from a short, often contorted or twisted, starchy, edible rootstock, terminating in a cluster of dark-green, shiny leaves. Stems up to 3 dm tall, terminating in a slender spike in which the lower flowers are replaced by bulbils. The white or pink flowers appear normal but rarely produce viable seeds. Reproduction therefore is mainly vegetative by the bulbils, which often commence growth while still attached to the mother plant. Common except in very damp places. Circumpolar, arctic-alpine.

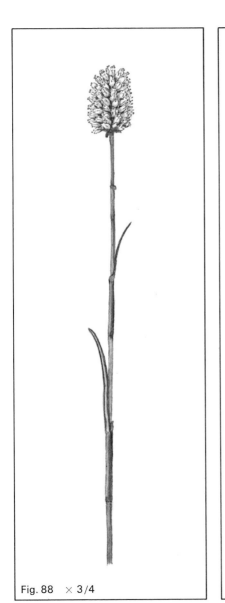

Fig. 88 × 3/4

Fig. 89 × 3/4

# CHENOPODIACEAE
**Goosefoot Family**

*Chenopodium capitatum* (L.) Aschers.
**Strawberry Blite**
Fig. 90

Annual. Stems simple or branching from the base, 2 to 4 dm tall, with alternate, somewhat succulent, dark-green leaves. Flowers in stalkless, spherical, clustered flower-heads, forming an interrupted spike; in fruit the clustered flower-heads becoming bright red, berry-like, and juicy. When cooked, the young leaves and stems make an acceptable substitute for spinach. Of weedy habit; occasional in wet places by roadsides and along trails. The bright red juice squeezed from the fruits was formerly used by Indians for war paint.

Fig. 90   × 2/3

# PORTULACACEAE
## Purslane Family

A small family in the area, represented by two species in the genus *Claytonia* and one in *Lewisia*. All are smooth perennials with corms or fleshy taproots; succulent alternate or opposite leaves; and perfect, regular flowers. Only the first is common; the remaining two are among the rarest species in the area.

*Claytonia lanceolata* Pursh
## Spring Beauty
Fig. 91

Stems 5 to 15 cm high, from a globose, 1-cm-thick, easily detached corm; basal leaves mostly one or two with oblong-lanceolate blade; the two stem-leaves opposite, stalkless, and broadly lanceolate; flowers in terminal, few-flowered racemes. The two sepals persistent, the four petals rose-coloured with purple veins. Common above timberline in moist herbmats, where it flowers early and wilts as soon as the one-celled, three-valved capsules mature. Cordilleran.

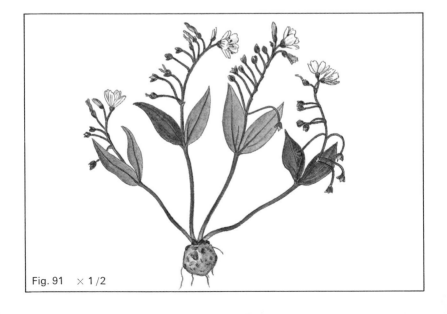

Fig. 91   × 1/2

*Claytonia megarrhiza* (Gray) Parry
**Thick-rooted Spring Beauty**
Fig. 92

Extremely rare and local in moist shaly places on high mountains. Cordilleran.

*Lewisia pygmaea* (Gray) Robins.
**Bitter Root**
Fig. 93

Rare and local in the southern parts of the area, where it has been collected only a few times near timberline. In life the elongated taproot is deeply buried in the soil, and the numerous linear leaves are spread flat on the ground. Cordilleran.

Fig. 92   × 2/5

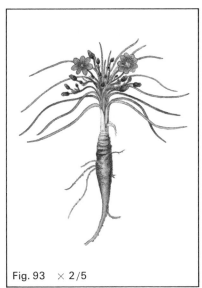

Fig. 93   × 2/5

## CARYOPHYLLACEAE
## Pink Family

Alpine members of family perennial with opposite undivided leaves and stems that are usually somewhat swollen at the nodes; flowers symmetrical, four- to five-parted, with or sometimes without petals; stamens usually twice the number of the sepals; styles two to five; fruit of alpine genera a several- to many-seeded capsule. Represented by eight genera with about three dozen species.

*Arenaria capillaris* Poir. ssp. *americana* Maguire
## Sandwort
Fig. 94

Densely tufted, 15 to 20 cm tall from a somewhat woody, branching rootstock; leaves thread-like, in clusters around the base of flowering stems that are somewhat sticky above. Common on dry rocky slopes. Cordilleran.

*Arenaria obtusiloba* Rydb. is much branched from a somewhat woody base, with decumbent-ascending, leafy, glandular-hairy stems 4 to 5 cm high; the leaves linear, obtuse, 2 to 5 mm long, and the flowers solitary or two or three together. Very rare, on alpine slopes along the Continental Divide. Cordilleran.

Ross's sandwort (*Arenaria Rossii* R. Br.) forms small, flat, reddish green tussocks with mostly solitary flowers commonly lacking petals, on short, slender stalks. High-alpine tundra and moraines. North America; high arctic, alpine.

Creeping sandwort (*Arenaria humifusa* Wahlenb.) is a smooth dwarf species with slender, creeping rootstocks and small tufts of tiny, somewhat fleshy leaves; the flowers solitary. Moist sand by alpine ponds and in rock crevices. North America; arctic-alpine.

Fig. 94   × 1/1

*Cerastium Earlei* Rydb.
**Mouse-Ear Chickweed**
Fig. 95

Loosely tufted or matted with simple or branched, fresh green, glandular-hairy stems and leaves. Alpine tundra and rocky slopes above timberline. Cordilleran.

Field chickweed (*Cerastium arvense* L.) is tufted, 15 to 20 cm tall, with linear-lanceolate, greyish green leaves in axillary clusters. Flowers in a terminal flat-topped cluster, the white petals two or three times longer than the sepals. Dry rocky screes and grassy slopes. Circumpolar.

Fig. 95  × 5/4

*Melandrium attenuatum* (Farr) Hara
**Bladder-Campion**
Fig. 96

Stems glandular-hairy, one to several, 10 to 15 cm tall, from a stout taproot ; flowers solitary, nodding ; the glandular-hairy, bladder-like calyx resembling a miniature Japanese lantern ; the small petals purplish and well exserted beyond the calyx. Common locally on alpine sliderock slopes and always on non-calcareous soil. Cordilleran.

The arctic bladder-campion, *Melandrium affine* (J. Vahl) Hartm., is somewhat similar, but the flowering stems are stouter, up to 3 dm tall, and the one to three flowers are erect ; their calyx is much less inflated. Rare in alpine tundra. North America ; arctic.

In the still taller bladder-campion, *Melandrium Drummondii* (Hook.) Porsild, the inflorescence is many-flowered ; the flowers are on long, erect stalks, the calyx narrowly cylindrical with green rather than purple stripes. The seeds are less than 1 mm in diameter and wingless, whereas those of the preceding species are twice as large and distinctly wing-margined. North America ; prairie and foothill species that barely enters the Rocky Mountain parks.

Fig. 96 × 1/2

*Silene acaulis* L.
**Moss Campion**
Fig. 97

Forms flat or slightly domed, firm cushions, sometimes attaining a diameter of up to 1 m. The stems are covered by short, flat leaves, each terminating in a single pinkish purple or, rarely, white flower. Common in stony or turfy places, mainly above timberline. Circumpolar, arctic-alpine.

Parry's campion, *Silene Parryi* (Wats.) Hitchc. & Maguire, is tufted from a short, somewhat woody base; flowering stems 2 to 3 dm tall with two or three pairs of leaves; inflorescence flat-topped of three to seven flowers, the calyx tubular, with ten greenish purple nerves. The calyx and the upper part of the stem are densely covered with short, glandular hairs in which small insects are often seen trapped. Presumably this sticky barrier is a protective measure against insects that are unable to pollinate the flowers because of their small size and are therefore not welcome visitors. Common locally on dry subalpine slopes. Cordilleran.

Fig. 97 × 1/1

*Stellaria longipes* Goldie
**Chickweed**
Fig. 98

Erect-decumbent, matted or, in exposed places, even densely tufted perennial. Leaves blue-green, stiff, linear-lanceolate, usually broadest below the middle. Flowers terminal or axillary, solitary or in few-flowered cymes. Fruit a shiny black capsule, opening by six valves.

*Stellaria longipes* is represented in the area by four or five not always easily separated minor species or races. Most common of these in alpine situations is *Stellaria monantha* Hult.

*Stellaria calycantha* Bong. is pale yellowish green, with weak and simple or branched stems; the flowers are long-stalked, single from the upper leaf-axils. Common in alpine herbmats and meadows. Nearly circumboreal.

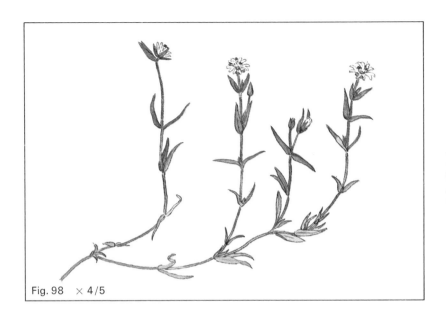

Fig. 98 × 4/5

*Stellaria umbellata* Turcz.
**Umbrella Chickweed**
Fig. 99

Stems slender, 15 to 25 cm tall, smooth, simple or branching above, from a creeping, thread-like rootstock. Inflorescence terminal, of small green flowers lacking petals, in one or several umbels. In wet places by alpine brooks or by seepages. Northwestern America and eastern Asia.

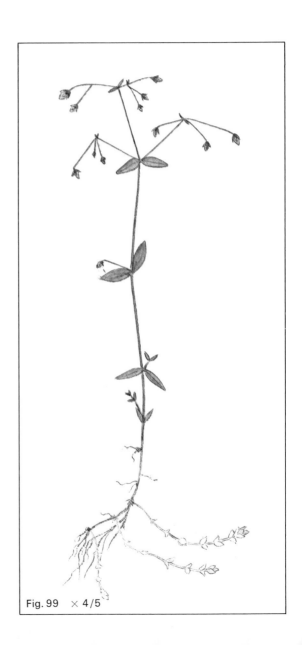

Fig. 99   × 4/5

## RANUNCULACEAE
## Crowfoot Family

Here mainly perennial herbs (except the vine *Clematis*) with acrid juice and alternate simple or compound leaves, mainly without stipules but often with the leaf-stalk dilated at the base. Flowers mostly regular and symmetrical, petals numerous or sometimes lacking, with petal-like calyx and numerous stamens; the carpels numerous, few or solitary; fruit an achene or a many-seeded pod, rarely berry-like.

A large but technically not too critical family, here represented by 11 genera with a total of nearly 60 species, of which 23 are in the genus *Ranunculus*.

*Actaea arguta* Nutt.
## Red Baneberry
Fig. 100

Stems erect, 5 to 10 dm high, from a thick, branching rootstock. Leaves large, once or twice three-parted, thin and fresh green, the lower long-petioled, the upper stalkless. Flowers small, in terminal racemes; the petal-like, early-deciduous sepals creamy white; petals smaller and inconspicuous. Fruit berry-like containing a few large seeds, commonly coral red. Occasionally growing together with an ivory-white fruited form (*Actaea eburnea* Rydb.); the fruits of both said to be poisonous. Damp clearings in forest. Cordilleran north to southern Alaska.

Fig. 100    × 2/3

*Anemone Drummondii* S. Wats.
**Drummond's Anemone**
Fig. 101

Tufted, 2-to-3-dm-tall perennial. Leaf-blades silky-hirsute, with narrow, linear segments. Flowers solitary, tinged with blue, commonly less than 3 cm in diameter. Fruiting heads globose; achenes densely woolly, with a straight, slender style. Common above timberline in open heath and herbmats. Cordilleran alpine, north to the Yukon and Alaska.

*Anemone parviflora* Michx. has a slender rootstock, larger, commonly bluish-tinged flowers and three-parted leaves with broadly wedge-shaped segments; achenes woolly, in a globose head. Common in open sandy or gravelly places from lowland floodplains to above timberline. North America and eastern Asia; arctic-alpine.

Cut-leaved anemone (*Anemone multifida* Poir.) is densely tufted with stems up to 45 cm tall; leaves densely silky-pubescent; the flowers smaller, one to three, white or tinged with pink; woolly in a globose head. Dry grassy slopes and meadows of the lowland. North America.

Fig. 101   × 1/1

*Aquilegia flavescens* S. Wats.
**Yellow Columbine**
Fig. 102

Flowering stems 2 to 6 dm high. Flowers ill-scented, large, pale yellow, nodding ; the sepals petal-like and the blade of the petals prolonged into a slender, hollow spur. Fruit a many-seeded hairy pod. Common locally on acid rocky ledges and screes to and slightly above timberline.

The similar but red-flowered columbine, *Aquilegia formosa* Fisch., grows mainly in moist alpine meadows. *Aquilegia brevistyla* Hook. with blue sepals and white petals is a boreal forest species that has been collected a few times in the northern parts of the area. Both North America.

Fig. 102 × 2/3

*Caltha leptosepala* DC.
## White-flowered Marsh-Marigold
Fig. 103

Perennial from a short, erect rootstock, with fresh green, somewhat fleshy, heart-shaped leaves and pinkish, naked flowering stems, each with one or two flowers. Sepals white, commonly tinged with blue; petals wanting. Fruiting heads top-shaped of several many-seeded pods. Common in wet alpine and subalpine meadows. Cordilleran.

Fig. 103   × 2/3

*Clematis columbiana* T. & G.
**Purple Virgin's Bower**
Fig. 104

Woody creeping vine with solitary large flowers; sepals pale purple or blue, petals small, inconspicuous, or wanting; seeds numerous, the persistent style long and plumose. Creeping over fallen logs or rocks, in open thickets. Cordilleran.

The smaller and more southern *Clematis ligusticifolia* Nutt., with pinnately dissected leaves and small, white flowers in a paniculate inflorescence, has been collected in Waterton Lakes Park.

Fig. 104 × 3/4

*Delphinium bicolor* Nutt.
**Dwarf Larkspur**
Fig. 105

Stems few-leaved, 2 to 4 dm tall from a short, branching rootstock. Inflorescence few-flowered ; sepals dark blue, petals greyish brown with blue veins. Pods glandular-hairy or smooth. Dry grassy slopes and meadows, often growing along sheep trails.

*Delphinium depauperatum* Nutt. is very similar but has tuber-like roots. Common locally in dry meadows. Both Cordilleran.

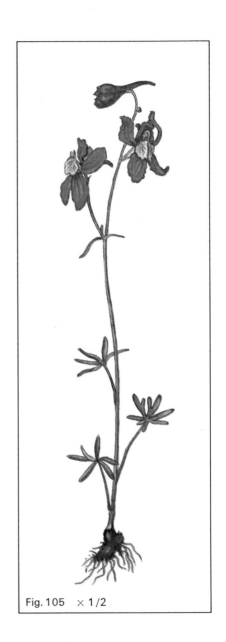

Fig. 105  × 1/2

*Delphinium glaucum* S. Wats.
**Tall Larkspur**
Fig. 106

Stems leafy, up to 2 m tall from a thick, somewhat woody rootstock.
Leaves mostly cauline, stalked, the blade palmately divided. Flowers
very numerous, dark purplish blue, in terminal lax-flowered raceme.
Fruit a many-seeded pod. Moist places in open woods and clearings or
along avalanche paths ; ascending to timberline. Northwestern America.

Fig. 106 × 4/5

*Pulsatilla Ludoviciana* (Nutt.) Heller
**Prairie Crocus or Pasque Flower**
Fig. 107

One of the earliest spring flowers in the mountains. In late May or early June when the snow is still melting on dry open slopes, the large, showy flowers appear. The leaves, silvery-white from dense, appressed pubescence, follow. As the nutlets mature, their persistent styles lengthen into feathery "tails" by which they become airborne by the lightest breeze. The prairie crocus is actually a true anemone and is not related to the crocus. Cordilleran foothills and plains north through Mackenzie District to the Arctic Coast, the Yukon, and eastern Alaska.

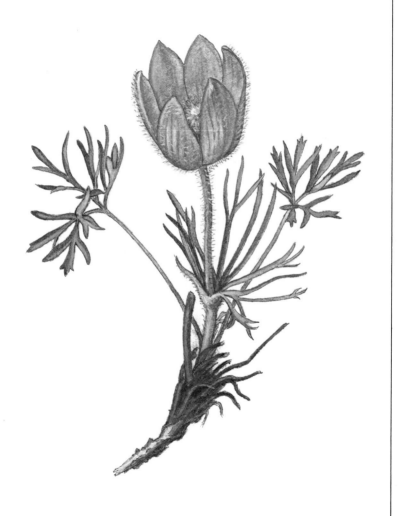

Fig. 107 × 4/5

*Pulsatilla occidentalis* (S. Wats.) Freyn
**White Pasque Flower**
Fig. 108

Perhaps the showiest of the true alpines; found mainly above timberline, where it is often dominant on moist slopes and in hollows where the snow remains late. The flowers appear before the leaves and actually commence growth beneath the snow, pushing their pale expanding heads through the crust. As the snow melts, the large flower expands rapidly, and soon after, the young silky leaves appear. A week or so later the plant is fully developed when the expanded, feathery, green leaves lose their silky hairs. In the fruiting state the white pasque flowers are known colloquially as "towhead babies", an allusion to the fuzzy appearance of the fruiting heads with their long, feathery, long-lasting styles that later serve as "parachutes" in the dispersal of the achenes. Cordilleran.

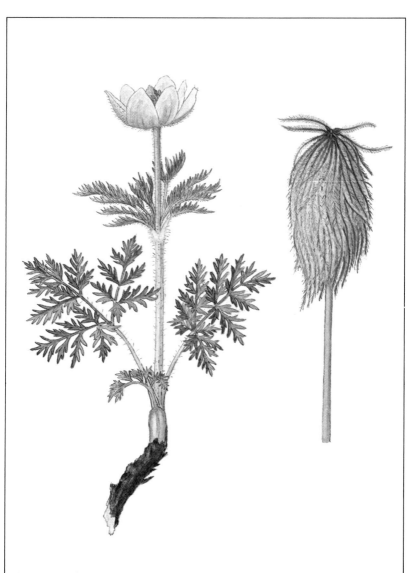

Fig. 108 × 2/3

*Ranunculus Eschscholtzii* Schlecht.
**Eschscholtz's Buttercup**
Fig. 109

Perhaps the commonest member of the buttercup tribe in the area, where it is found mainly above timberline on rather moist snowbed slopes and hollows. Common also in the mountains of the Yukon and Alaska.

*Ranunculus gelidus* Kar. & Kir. is a tufted dwarf species with ascending flowering stems often only 5 to 6 cm high, small, yellow flowers, and twice-divided, blue-green, smooth leaves; it grows on wet gravelly places far above timberline, but appears to be rare and local throughout its extensive range from Colorado over the Yukon and Alaska to mountains of central Asia.

Northern buttercup (*Ranunculus pedatifidus* Sm.), also tufted but taller, with palmately divided basal leaves, is wide-ranging arctic-alpine, although common also in foothill meadows.

Seaside buttercup (*Ranunculus cymbalaria* Pursh), with small, somewhat fleshy, kidney-shaped leaves and widely trailing runners rooting freely at the nodes, is often abundant locally along wet saline or alkaline pond margins.

Fig. 109   × 2/3

*Thalictrum occidentale* Gray
**Meadow Rue**
Fig. 110

Perennial, 5 to 10 dm tall from a stout rootstock ; leaves alternate, three-parted, glandular beneath ; flowers small, with greenish white sepals but lacking petals ; stamens with large, drooping anthers on thread-like filaments ; achenes stalkless, spindle-shaped. Common in damp alpine or subalpine meadows. Cordilleran.

*Thalictrum venulosum* Trel. is similar but taller ; the leaves are smooth and prominently veined beneath, and the achenes are shorter and thicker. Both are dioecious, that is, with distinct male and female plants. Common in open aspen woods, but not alpine.

Fig. 110 × 2/3

*Trollius albiflorus* (A. Gray) Salisb.
**White Globe-Flower**
Fig. 111

Flowers solitary or, rarely, two from the same stem ; sepals five to seven, petal-like, creamy white, often bluish-tinged on the outside ; petals five to eight, small and tubular at the base of the sepals. Fruiting head top-shaped, composed of several many-seeded pods. Common in wet alpine meadows and along alpine and subalpine brooks, often growing in masses with the white marsh-marigold and Eschscholtz's buttercup. Cordilleran.

Fig. 111 × 1/2

# BERBERIDACEAE
## Barberry Family

*Berberis repens* Lindl.
## Oregon Grapes
Fig. 112

Creeping dwarf shrub with three to seven pinnately compound, prickly toothed, evergreen leaflets. Flowers yellow, in many-flowered raceme. Fruit berry-like, dark blue, with a bloom. Open sunny slopes in Waterton Lakes Park. Cordilleran.

Fig. 112 × 4/5

# PAPAVERACEAE
## Poppy Family

*Papaver pygmaeum* Rydb.
## Dwarf Poppy
Fig. 113

Dwarf species with sparingly bristly or smooth, bluish green, 2-to-3-cm-long leaves, and small flowers on 4-to-6-cm-high scapes. The four petals orange or pale pink, 1 cm long or less. Capsule obovoid, about 1 cm long. Rare and local in rather moist sandy or gravelly places above timberline. Cordilleran.

Arctic poppy (*Papaver radicatum* Rottb.) is similar, but larger; leaves densely soft-hairy, 10 to 15 cm high; flowers larger with sulphur-yellow petals 1 to 2 cm long. Very rare, in stony and rocky places far above timberline. In a broad sense the arctic poppy is circumpolar but has been divided into a number of often narrowly limited geographic races.

Fig. 113 × 5/4

## FUMARIACEAE
**Fumitory Family**

*Corydalis aurea* Willd.
**Golden Corydalis**
Fig. 114

Smooth and somewhat succulent, blue-green biennial with diffusely branching, erect-ascending leafy stems, and alternate, two-parted leaves. Flowers perfect, irregular, in elongating racemes; fruit an elongated, two-valved pod. Sandy or gravelly riverbanks and slopes, mainly of lower elevations. North America.

Fig. 114  × 1/1

## CRUCIFERAE
## Mustard Family

Herbs with bitter, watery juice, and regular flowers with four deciduous sepals, four petals, and six stamens. Fruit in alpine species a two-valved pod (silique) ; the leaves alternate and without stipules ; the flowers in terminal racemes or corymbs. The family is represented here by 11 genera and about 50 species, of which about 21 are in the genus *Draba* and 11 in *Arabis*.

The alpine Drabas are perennial, mostly low or tufted, mostly stellate-pubescent herbs with entire or toothed leaves, white or yellow flowers, and flat elliptic or ovate pods one to three times as long as broad.

Rock cress (*Arabis*) is taller, with larger sub-entire or toothed leaves, erect-ascending or decumbent flowering stems, and linear pods six to twenty times as long as broad. Only a few members of the genus are truly alpine.

*Arabis Lyallii* S. Wats.
## Rock Cress
Fig. 115

Stems leafy, 15 to 25 cm tall from a branching taproot ; leaves fresh green and smooth ; the few large flowers pale purple, the stiffly erect pods 4 to 5 cm long and 2 to 3 mm wide ; the seeds in two rows. Moist alpine slopes and herbmats. Cordilleran.

*Arabis Lemmonii* S. Wats. of high-alpine slopes differs by its narrower, usually curved and horizontally spreading pods with seeds in one row.

Two others, *Arabis divaricarpa* and *A. retrofracta*, are biennial or short-lived perennials and grow on dry, sunny slopes or river terraces, but are not truly alpine. Both are grey from close pubescence, and their stems are commonly branching, their pods 5 to 7 cm long, spreading in *Arabis divaricarpa* and pendulous in *A. retrofracta*.

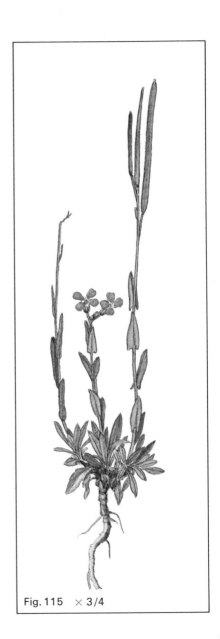

Fig. 115 × 3/4

*Cardamine bellidifolia* L.
**Bitter Cress**
Fig. 116

Dwarf tufted perennial with branched stems and mostly basal, smooth, deep-green leaves and small, white flowers. Pods stiffly erect, linear, 2 to 2.5 cm long, their valves black when mature. Moist rocky crevices, often shaded, and places where the snow remains late. Circumpolar, high alpine.

Bladder-pod, *Lesquerella arctica* (Wormskj.) Wats. ssp. *Purshii* (Wats.) Porsild, is a silvery, hairy perennial with a stout taproot and rosette of oblanceolate leaves tapering into a slender leafstalk; the flowering stems erect-ascending, 5 to 20 cm tall, and the pale yellow flowers in an elongating raceme; pods globular or somewhat pear-shaped, about 4 mm in diameter, on ascending peduncles 1 to 2 cm long.

*Draba incerta* Payson
Fig. 117

Loosely tufted; leaves linear-oblanceolate with a prominent midrib, mainly basal, hairy with variously branched hairs mainly on the underside. Flowering stems 10 to 12 cm tall, the inflorescence open, soon elongating; flowers bright yellow, scented; pods elliptic, 6 to 8 mm long, on stalks two to three times as long as the pod. Very common in alpine tundra, rocky crevices, and moist gravelly places. Cordilleran.

Fig. 116 × 3/4

Fig. 117 × 2/3

*Draba oligosperma* Hook.
Fig. 118

Densely tufted ; leaves linear, densely overlapping, with prominent midvein, loosely covered by simple or branched hairs. Flowering stems 5 to 10 cm tall, elongating in fruit ; flowers pale yellow ; pods ovoid, not much flattened, sparingly pubescent or glabrous, 4 to 5 mm long. Dry, sunny cliffs. Cordilleran.

Most common in the area among the white-flowered, scapose species is the arctic *Draba nivalis*, which is densely tufted with the basal leaves grey from finely stellate hairs. Flowers small ; pods linear-lanceolate, smooth.

Among the leafy-stemmed species, *Draba aurea* and *D. luteola* have pale yellow flowers, whereas *Draba glabella*, *D. praealta*, and *D. lanceolata* have white flowers. *Draba crassifolia* and *D. nitida* are winter annuals ; the first with pale yellow flowers, the second with white flowers.

*Draba ventosa* Gray
Fig. 119

Low and loosely tufted from a generally much branched base ; leaves basal, overlapping, somewhat fleshy, stellate-pubescent. Scapes 3 to 6 cm tall, inflorescence short, not elongating in fruit ; petals bright yellow ; pods short, elliptical, stellate-pubescent, with a prominent style. On moist, gravelly sliderock on high mountains. Very local and rare. Cordilleran.

Fig. 118  × 2/3

Fig. 119  × 2/3

*Smelowskia calycina* C. A. Mey. var. *americana* (Rydb.) Drury & Rollins
Fig. 120

Tufted, blue-grey, hairy perennial from a branched ascending stem, usually deeply buried in sliderock, the branches densely covered by persistent leaf-bases. Basal leaves oblanceolate, entire or notched, those of the stem pinnately divided ; the small, white flowers in a terminal raceme, which elongates as the narrowly oblong and keeled, 7-to-12-mm-long pods mature. High-alpine sliderock slopes. Cordilleran.

*Erysimum Pallasii* (Pursh) Fern. is a biennial or short-lived perennial, which, after two to several years in the rosette stage, flowers, matures seeds, and dies. The leaves are linear-lanceolate, 5 to 7 cm long, and the inflorescence terminal in a rapidly elongating raceme of up to 50 large, purple, very fragrant flowers. The pods 4 to 11 cm long and 2 to 3 mm wide, usually somewhat curved. Very rare and local, in high-alpine rocky places. Circumpolar, high arctic.

Fig. 120   × 4/5

CRASSULACEAE
**Stonecrop Family**

*Rhodiola integrifolia* Raf.
**Rose-Root**
Fig. 121

Succulent, dioecious perennial with a fleshy branching rootstock, each branch terminating in a leafy stem 10 to 15 cm high. Flowers in terminal clusters ; those of the male plant usually yellow but always purple in the female plant ; pods plump, erect, reddish purple. Rare, in moist rocky or gravelly places above timberline. Northwestern America and eastern Asia. Arctic-alpine.

*Sedum lanceolatum* Torr.
**Stonecrop**
Fig. 122

Tufted, succulent perennial from a slender, freely branching rootstock ; the terminal branch 10 to 15 cm high with a cluster of yellow flowers, the lateral and leafy branches sterile ; pods erect with spreading, persistent styles. Common on dry sunny slopes and screes ; ascending to far above timberline. Cordilleran, ranging north to the southern Yukon.

Fig. 121 × 1/2

Fig. 122 × 4/5

# SAXIFRAGACEAE
## Saxifrage Family

Alpine members of the family perennial, mainly with regular, perfect
five-parted (in *Chrysosplenium* four-parted) flowers; petals as many
as the sepals, or wanting; stamens as many, or twice as many, as the
sepals; styles two or three. Fruit a capsule or berry. In the parks represented by 12 genera with a total of 50-odd species, of which 20 are
in the genus *Saxifraga*.

*Heuchera ovalifolia* Nutt.
## Alum Root
Fig. 123

Perennial from a thick, scaly, somewhat woody rootstock. Leaves
somewhat leathery, glandular-hairy, all basal, their blades 2 to 4 cm
broad, oval or heart-shaped. Scapes densely glandular-hairy. Inflorescence spike-like, of small, yellowish-green flowers that usually lack
petals. Dry, sunny rocky slopes, ascending to or slightly above timberline. Cordilleran.

*Leptarrhena pyrolifolia* (D. Don) Ser.
## Leather-leaved Saxifrage
Fig. 124

Perennial from a horizontal, branched rootstock; often of somewhat
matted growth. Leaves mainly basal, leathery. Flowering stems 1 to
4 dm high; flowers small, in few-flowered clusters; petals white.
Common locally in wet places by alpine brooks and by the edge of
alpine herbmats. Mainly along the Continental Divide. Alaska–Yukon
Territory south to British Columbia and Washington.

Fig. 123   × 1/3

Fig. 124   × 1/3

*Lithophragma parviflora* (Hook.) Nutt.
**Star-Flower**
Fig. 125

Slender, glandular-hairy perennial, with a leafy flowering stem 1 to 3 dm high from a thin, bulblet-bearing rootstock. Fruit a three-valved capsule. Rare and local, on dry grassy slopes, often by game trails at the head of screes, or by animal burrows. Cordilleran.

*Mitella nuda* L.
**Mitrewort**
Fig. 126

Dwarf perennial with slender, creeping rootstock; leaves all basal, the blade roundish with crenate margins, soft-hairy on both sides; scapes 10 to 15 cm tall, flowers greenish, in few-flowered raceme, the comb-like dissected petals twice as long as the sepals. Fruit a two-valved capsule containing small, shiny, black seeds. Cold coniferous woods and bogs, mainly at lower elevations. Boreal North America and eastern Asia.

*Mitella pentandra* Hook. has a stouter rootstock and flowering stems 1 to 3 dm tall, and more numerous flowers. Rather common in alpine herbmats near or slightly above timberline. Cordilleran, reaching the southern Yukon and Alaska.

Fig. 125 × 2/3

Fig. 126 × 1/1 (× 4/1)

*Parnassia fimbriata* Koenig
**Grass-of-Parnassus**
Fig. 127

Tufted, smooth perennial from short, ascending rootstock. Scapes 2 to 4 dm tall, with a single small leaf. Flower solitary, the petals fringed at base and the five fertile stamens alternating with five gland-tipped sterile ones. Fruit a many-seeded, four-valved capsule. Very common in snowbed herbmats at or above timberline. Cordilleran but reaching the southwestern Yukon and Alaska.

The arctic-alpine *Parnassia Kotzebuei* C. & S. is also common above timberline, where it usually grows in wet places by alpine brooks or by ponds. It is smaller, with scapes rarely over 10 to 15 cm tall ; its basal leaves are oval, and the non-fringed petals scarcely longer than the sepals. North America.

Fig. 127   × 2/3

*Ribes cereum* Lindl.
**Wild Currant**
Fig. 128

Much branched, low and unarmed shrub, 1 m high or less. Flowers white or pink, in short racemes. Berries bright red, smooth. Subalpine slopes and clearings, barely entering the area along the Continental Divide. Western Cordilleran.

Fig. 128   × 2/3

*Ribes lacustre* (Pers.) Poir.
**Swamp Currant**
Fig. 129

Low, straggling shrub with spiny, bristly stems up to 1 m high. The small, green, pink, or purplish flowers in drooping racemes. Berries purplish, densely glandular-bristly. Common in open places in woods, on slopes, and along trails, to or slightly above timberline. North America.

Skunk currant (*Ribes glandulosum* Grauer) is a straggling shrub up to 1 m tall, lacking spines or bristles; leaves thin, deeply five- to seven-lobed, ill-smelling when rubbed; flowers pale pink or white in long, erect racemes; berries red, glandular, bristly. Common in damp woods.

*Saxifraga adscendens* L. ssp. *oregonensis* (Raf.) Bacigalupi
Fig. 130

Glandular-hairy biennial or short-lived perennial with a small basal rosette and a leafy, simple or branched flowering stem 10 to 15 cm tall. Occasional to common by alpine brooks and in wet rock crevices. Northwestern America; alpine.

Fig. 129 × 4/5

Fig. 130 × 1/2

*Saxifraga aizoides* L.
**Yellow Mountain Saxifrage**
Fig. 131

Low and matted ; stems decumbent, ascending with somewhat spread-ing, linear, fleshy leaves, terminating in a few-flowered raceme ; petals yellow and mostly orange-dotted. Common on moist sand and gravel, ascending to far above timberline. Amphi-Atlantic, arctic-alpine.

Fig. 131 × 4/3

*Saxifraga bronchialis* L. ssp. *austromontana* (Wieg.) Piper
**Prickly Saxifrage**
Fig. 132

Densely matted with copiously leafy, branching stems. Leaves leathery, narrowly lanceolate, fringed with long hairs, terminating in a sharp spine. Peduncles 10 to 15 cm tall, leafy ; petals white, prominently spotted with yellow. Common on not too dry cliffs and in somewhat shaded crevices, ascending from valley slopes to well above timberline. Cordilleran.

Rather similar and sometimes confused with it is the arctic *Saxifraga tricuspidata* Rottb., in which the leaves are distinctly three-toothed, each tooth terminating in a short spine. North America ; arctic-alpine south in the mountains to Jasper Park.

Fig. 132 × 1/1

*Saxifraga cernua* L.
**Nodding Saxifrage**
Fig. 133

Stem slender, erect, simple, and leafy, 10 to 25 cm high, with a cluster of white bulblets hidden at base. Blades of the basal and lower stem-leaves kidney-shaped, three- to five-lobed, the upper stem-leaves reduced and subtending clusters of small, reddish purple bulbils. The single terminal flower is large and nodding in youth. Circumpolar, wide-ranging, arctic-alpine.

Fig. 133    × 1/1

*Saxifraga flagellaris* Willd.
**Spider Plant**
Fig. 134

Stems single, erect, leafy, and glandular, 3 to 15 cm high from a small basal rosette, from which radiate whip-like, naked runners, each terminating in a tiny rooting offset. The vernacular name of this plant refers to its spider-like appearance. It is one of the rarest plants in the area, where it is known only from a single station at an elevation of 9,000 ft. Circumpolar and high arctic, alpine.

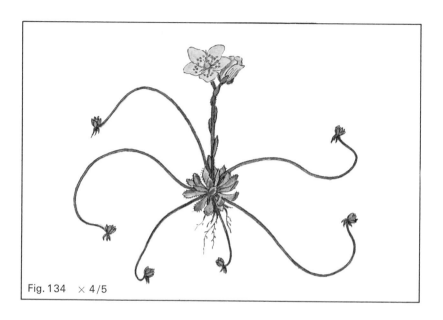

Fig. 134 × 4/5

*Saxifraga Lyallii* Engler
Fig. 135

Flowering scapes 2 to 3 dm tall from an elongated, ascending root-stock, terminating in a cluster of wedge-shaped, toothed leaves. A most attractive species, often growing in dense masses in wet moss by alpine brooks or by seepages. Northwestern America.

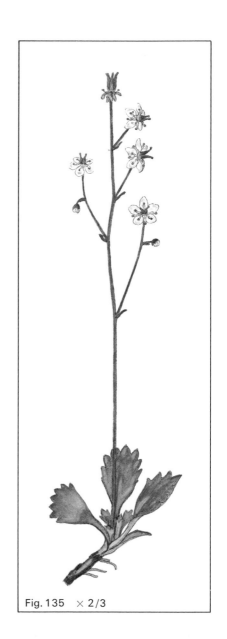

Fig. 135 ✕ 2/3

*Saxifraga oppositifolia* L.
**Purple Saxifrage**
Fig. 136

Densely or loosely matted with crowded or trailing branches and overlapping scale-like, four-ranked, persistent and bristly-ciliated leaves. Flowers purple, solitary on short stalks. Common above timberline, mostly in damp gravelly places. Circumpolar, arctic-alpine.

The Cordilleran tufted saxifrage, *Saxifraga caespitosa* L. ssp. *monticola* (Small) Porsild, forms small, soft cushions of numerous crowded, leafy branches; the individual leaves wedge-shaped, three- or, rarely, five-lobed.

Flowering stems slender, erect, 5 to 10 cm high. Flowers one to three in small, dense clusters, the petals white or pale pink, and the calyx top-shaped and black, glandular-hirsute. Common on rocky ledges near or above timberline.

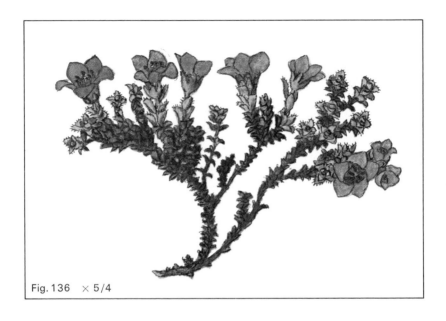

Fig. 136    × 5/4

# ROSACEAE
## Rose Family

Herbs, shrubs or, rarely, small trees, with simple or compound, alternate and stipulate leaves. Flowers five-parted, regular and perfect, with a united calyx and free petals. Fruit a dry achene, pod, or a drupe or berry containing several seeds. A large family ; represented in the area by 16 genera and about 70 species, of which nearly half are in the genus *Potentilla*.

*Amelanchier alnifolia* Nutt.
**Alder-leaved Service-Berry**
Fig. 137

At low elevations shrub-like and 1 to 3 m tall, but in the alpine zone low and straggling. The white flowers appearing in June soon after the leaves begin to unfold. The sweet, juicy fruits resembling blueberries in appearance and taste ; formerly used dried as a substitute for raisins, and by the Indians for seasoning buffalo pemmican. In the mountains the only common member of this large and taxonomically difficult genus.

Fig. 137 × 1/1

*Dryas Drummondii* Richards.
**Yellow Mountain Avens**
Fig. 138

This very handsome species is at once distinguished from other members of the genus by its pale yellow, nodding flowers that are never fully expanded, on scapes 15 to 25 cm tall. In fruit it is even showier when the young styles become twisted into a shiny, golden-yellow top.

Commonly pioneering on gravelly floodplains where, in the absence of competition, individual plants spread radially to form circular "islands" up to 2 or 3 m in diameter. The yellow avens does not reach the alpine zone but extends north along the valleys of the Mackenzie and Yukon Rivers, and in the East has isolated outposts on the north shore of Lake Superior and in the region of the Gulf of St. Lawrence.

Fig. 138　× 1/1

*Dryas Hookeriana* Juz.
**White-flowered Mountain Avens**
Fig. 139

Dwarf shrub with trailing, freely rooting, leafy stems, often forming large, flat cushions in calcareous, gravelly, or stony places, mainly above timberline. It is endemic to the Rocky Mountains and, like other members of the genus, is intolerant of shade and competition. The leathery, coarsely serrated leaves are dark green and wrinkled above, and the underside is covered by a dense, white felt. Soon after flowering, the persistent styles elongate into long, feathery "tails" that serve as "sails" in the spreading of the nutlets (achenes).

*Dryas integrifolia* Vahl, at once distinguished by its entire, often revolute-margined leaves that are smooth and somewhat shiny above, is wide-ranging in the North American Arctic from Greenland to Alaska, south to or slightly beyond the treeline; in the Rocky Mountains south to Jasper Park with isolated stations in Montana; and in the East with isolated stations on the north shore of Lake Superior, the Gaspé, and in the White Mountains of New Hampshire. Leaves preserved in peat bogs show that during the Ice Age *Dryas integrifolia* extended southward far beyond its present southern limit.

*Fragaria glauca* (S. Wats.) Rydb.
**Wild Strawberry**
Fig. 140

Rather similar to the cultivated strawberry, but flowers and fruits much smaller. The very sweet, juicy fruits are eaten by a number of birds and by small rodents and foxes, which, in turn, help to distribute the seeds. One of the commonest plants in the area from the lowlands to well beyond timberline, it is particularly abundant in places where the snow disappears early. Northwestern North America.

Fig. 139 × 1/1

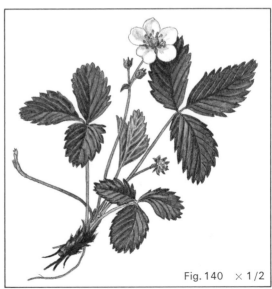

Fig. 140 × 1/2

*Geum triflorum* Pursh
**Old Man's Whiskers**
Fig. 141

Tufted perennial from a stout, somewhat woody rootstock. Leaves mainly basal, pinnate. Flowering stems 2 to 4 dm tall, stiff, minutely hairy, and bright pink or red; flowers usually three, at first nodding, the petals pinkish yellow; styles long and feathery, much elongated in fruit. Subalpine meadows and dry grassland. North America.

Fig. 141  × 1/2

*Luetkea pectinata* (Pursh) Kuntze
Fig. 142

Matted, evergreen dwarf shrub with prostrate, shallowly buried branches and leafy flowering stems 10 to 15 cm high. Leaves fan-shaped, the tiny blade divided into three-toothed lobes. Flowers small, regular, and white, in an elongating raceme. Fruit a many-seeded small pod. Alpine snowbed meadows, mainly on acid soil. Northwest American species very rare in the Alberta parks, where it has been collected only a few times along the Continental Divide.

*Potentilla diversifolia* Lehm.
**Cinquefoil**
Fig. 143

Tufted perennial from a stout, branched rootstock, with flowering stems 2.5 to 5 dm tall and three to five bright yellow flowers. In the area represented by two races, of which ssp. *glaucophylla* Lehm. with finger-shaped, five- to seven-parted, glabrous leaves is illustrated. In the very similar ssp. *diversifolia* the leaves are fresh green and silky-pubescent, and the first pair of leaflets is always somewhat remote from the rest. Both are common in alpine herbmats but are rarely found below timberline.

Fig. 142 × 1/1

Fig. 143 × 3/5

*Potentilla fruticosa* L.
**Shrubby Cinquefoil**
Fig. 144

Freely branching, erect or ascending, 3-to-15-dm-high, leafy shrub with brown, shreddy bark ; leaves with three to seven closely crowded leaflets ; the large, pale yellow flowers solitary or few together from leaf-axils near the tip of the branches. Common, generally on calcareous soils in a variety of habitats from gravelly river flats, dry meadows, or cliffs, to or slightly above timberline. Nearly circumpolar, subarctic-alpine.

The silverweed (*Potentilla anserina* L.) is tufted with oblanceolate, pinnately divided leaves composed of numerous leaflets, dark green above and silky-tomentose beneath, and its yellow flowers singly on a slender stalk. From the base of the plant issue long, whip-like runners, similar to those of the strawberry plant. Common on damp, alluvial river flats and lakeshores, but never in the alpine zone. Circumpolar.

Fig. 144　× 1/1

*Potentilla Ledebouriana* Porsild
Fig. 145

Densely tufted from a branching base ; the branches clothed by the remains of decaying leaf-stalks ; leaves mainly basal, deep green above with long, silky hair, white-tomentose beneath ; the flowers deep yellow, 1.5 to 2 cm in diameter. Forms large, compact cushions on dry rocky slopes, well above timberline. Eastern Asia and northwestern America ; arctic-alpine.

In this notoriously difficult genus, represented in the Alberta mountain parks by some 30 species, the leaves of *Potentilla Drummondii, P. Macounii, P. ovina,* and *P. rubricaulis* are composed of five or more leaflets, whereas in *P. concinna, P. fallax, P. hyparctica, P. nivea,* and *P. Ledebouriana* they are three-parted ; all are occasional to common above timberline.

Fig. 145 × 5/4

*Rosa Woodsii* Lindl.
**Wild Rose**
Fig. 146

Shrub commonly 5 to 15 dm tall; stems usually smooth between the rather stout, straight or curved thorns; leaflets commonly seven to nine; flowers usually in small clusters, or solitary on young plants. Common on dry grassy slopes, riverbanks, and clearings, mainly below timberline.

Equally common and in similar places is the prickly rose, *Rosa acicularis*, in which the leaflets are commonly in fives and the petals are a paler pink.

Fig. 146 × 1/1

*Rubus acaulis* Michx.
**Dewberry**
Fig. 147

Tiny herbaceous species with large, pink flowers. Its rather small fruits are sweet and aromatic and are considered a rare and exquisite treat by those few who have tasted them. Common in timberline forest and alpine tundra.

Fig. 147   × 1/1

*Rubus Chamaemorus* L.
**Cloudberry or Baked-Apple**
Fig. 148

This low herbaceous species of raspberry has been reported from the northern parts of Jasper Park, but its home is in sphagnum bogs of subarctic tundra. The single large, white flowers, unlike those of other members of the genus, are unisexual, on separate male and female plants. The large fruit is deep red when still unripe and becomes amber-yellow and very juicy when ripe.

Fig. 148　× 4/5

*Rubus parviflorus* Nutt.
**Thimbleberry**
Fig. 149

Erect or often trailing, unarmed shrub 1 to 2 m high, easily recognized by its up to 20-cm-broad, three- to five-lobed, deep-green leaves, its white flowers, and red, raspberry-like, but rather dry and tasteless fruits. A western species of wooded subalpine streambeds that barely enters the area along the Continental Divide, where it is a low, straggling shrub.

More common and widespread is the wild raspberry, *Rubus strigosus* Michx., which has prickly canes up to 2 m tall and is not unlike the garden raspberry. It is common in clearings and by roadsides but may be seen also on rocky, open, sunny screes or talus-slopes above timberline, where its fruits are harvested by chipmunks and other small rodents. The undigested seeds from their droppings start new growth, and it is for this reason, rather than by design, that wild raspberry plants often grow by their dens. Its fruits are smaller but taste like those of the cultivated variety.

*Sibbaldia procumbens* L.
Fig. 150

Dwarf perennial of matted growth, with freely branched rootstock terminating in clusters of three-parted, long-stalked leaves; flowers very small, pale yellow, in bracted, few-flowered heads barely overtopping the leaves. Common in alpine snowbed meadows. Circumpolar, alpine.

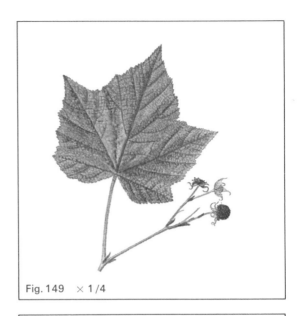

Fig. 149  × 1/4

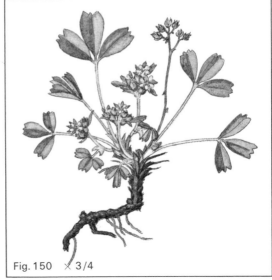

Fig. 150  × 3/4

# LEGUMINOSAE
## Pea Family

Alpine members of the family are perennial herbs with alternate,
compound, stipulate leaves; flowers perfect and irregular, of five
more or less united sepals and five unlike petals, of which the largest
and uppermost is called the standard, the two lateral and similar
the wings, and below them the keel, consisting of the two lowermost
and united petals; stamens ten, of which nine are united and only
one is free; fruit a variously shaped pod or legume. Roots commonly
with numerous tiny nodules containing nitrogen-fixing bacteria.

A large, very diverse family, but in the mountains represented by only
6 genera with a total of 40-odd species, of which three-fourths are in
*Astragalus* (milk-vetch) and *Oxytropis* (locoweed), and not very
many in the alpine zone. Although more than a dozen species of
milk-vetches are known from the Rocky Mountain parks of Alberta,
only a few are truly alpine; more are prairies species and are
restricted to the foothills and to intermontane grassland. Members of
the genera *Astragalus* and *Oxytropis* are not always easily placed in
their proper genus, except when in flower. In the *Astragalus* flower the
tip of the keel is always rounded; in *Oxytropis* it is sharply pointed.

*Astragalus alpinus* L.
## Alpine Milk-Vetch
Fig. 151

Low and matted with creeping, freely branched, weak stems. Leaflets
eight to eleven pairs, oblong-elliptic, with white, short, bristly hairs
beneath, smooth or sparingly appressed-hairy above. Flowering
stalks axillary, with a short, non-elongating raceme of pale bluish-
violet flowers. Pods pendulous and conspicuously black- or brownish-
hairy. Wide-ranging, circumpolar, arctic-alpine species, common
above and near timberline, often descending along valley streambeds.

*Astragalus eucosmus* Richards. is
another arctic-alpine species; it has
slender, erect-ascending leafy stems
from a somewhat woody rootstock. The
inflorescence of small, deep-purple
flowers is at first short but soon elongates; its small, obliquely ovoid, almost
stalkless, pendulous pods are densely
black-pubescent. Known only from a
few stations in Banff Park.

In the more common and somewhat
similar Richardson's milk-vetch (*Astragalus aboriginorum* Richards.) the
leaves are densely ashy-grey and tomentose, the flowers larger, pale pink or
yellowish white, and the distinctly
stalked pods much larger, smooth,
wine-red, and inflated.

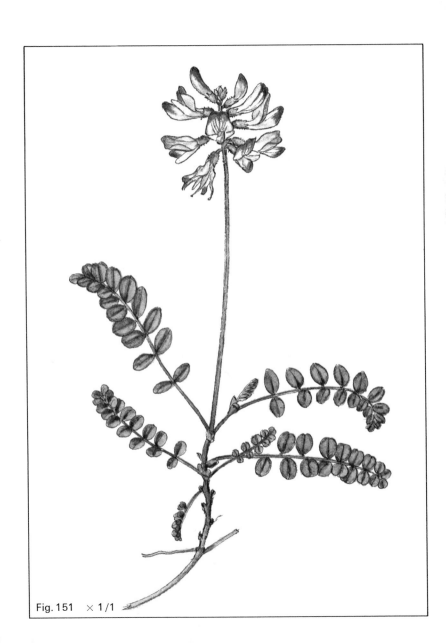

Fig. 151    × 1/1

*Astragalus miser* Dougl. ex Hook
Fig. 152

Stems tufted, slender and ascending, 1 to 3 dm tall from a slender, branching taproot. Leaflets nine to fifteen, linear and narrowly oblong, 7 to 12 mm long and 1.5 to 2 mm wide, grey-green and glabrous above and sparingly strigose beneath. Flowers small, pale purplish, in a narrow, elongating raceme; pods linear, glabrous or nearly so, 8 to 12 mm long. Said to be highly poisonous. A foothill species of open aspen or spruce woods.

*Astragalus Bourgovii* A. Gray has several slender and ascending stems, commonly 4 dm tall and freely branching from a strong, somewhat woody taproot, the leaflets linear-lanceolate. The flowers are small, dark purple, in an open few- to ten-flowered and elongating raceme; the pods are black, hairy, oblong, about 15 mm long. Cordilleran alpine species, common locally in gravelly places and often at the head of talus-slopes; on the Sunshine Plateau ascending to 8,200 ft.

Fig. 152   × 2/3

*Astragalus frigidus* (L.) Gray var. *americanus* (Hook.) Wats.
**American Milk-Vetch**
Fig. 153

This tallest of the alpine milk-vetches is common along alpine streams and brooks, where it often forms dense clumps. From a stout, somewhat woody base rise the fresh green, freely branched, up to 1-m-tall leafy stems. The small, pale, greenish white flowers are clustered at the end of a naked stalk from the upper leaf-axils; pods pale green and drooping. Cordilleran.

Fig. 153  × 4/5

*Astragalus striatus* Nutt.
**Milk-Vetch**
Fig. 154

Stems leafy and freely branched, erect or ascending, and commonly 4 dm tall from a strong, branched base ; leaflets dark green, 1 to 2 cm long. Inflorescence of numerous densely crowded, pale-purplish flowers in an elongating spike ; the pods oblong, 8 to 12 mm long, finely hairy. Cordilleran species common in dampish river meadows.

Fig. 154　× 2/3

*Hedysarum Mackenzii* Richards.
Fig. 155

Stems numerous, ascending or arching, 2 to 5 dm high, from a much branched, somewhat woody base and a thick, fibrous root; leaves with from five to seven pairs of silvery-grey leaflets; flowers five to fifteen, large, rose-purple and sweet-scented, in a very showy, elongating raceme; the legumes flat and jointed, transversely veined, separating at the narrow constrictions when ripe. Common; often forming colonies on well-watered, gravelly river flats, in Banff and Jasper Parks. North America and eastern Asia; arctic-alpine.

*Hedysarum alpinum* L. is at once distinguished from *H. Mackenzii* by its green, smooth leaves and its non-scented, smaller but more numerous, pale pink flowers and net-veined legumes. North America and eastern Asia; arctic-alpine.

*Hedysarum sulphurescens* Rydb. with its pale yellow flowers is a plant of open subalpine forest and thickets. Cordilleran.

Fig. 155   × 1/2

*Lupinus minimus* Dougl.
**Dwarf Lupine**
Fig. 156

A neat and very attractive dwarf species with silvery grey leaflets that are commonly folded lengthwise, and small, deep purplish-blue flowers in a dense, spike-like raceme barely raised above the leaves. A rare species in the Canadian Rocky Mountains, where it is known only from Waterton Lakes Park.

Fig. 156   × 2/3

*Oxytropis*
**Locoweed**

Perennial, mostly stemless herbs with alternate or odd-pinnate leaves
and flowers in a spike or raceme on a stiffly erect or ascending stalk
overtopping the leaves. Pods oblong or ovoid. About a dozen species
are known from the area but only a few ascend beyond timberline.

*Oxytropis podocarpa* A. Gray
**Bladder Locoweed**
Fig. 157

Densely tufted from a stout, fibrous, and often much branched taproot; leaves 2 to 3 cm long with five to seven pairs of tiny leaflets.
Flowers solitary or paired, about 2 cm long, barely overtopping the
leaves. Much more spectacular are the 2-to-3-cm-long, much
inflated, bright red or purple pods that become detached from their
stalks when ripe and are carried off by the wind. Cordilleran alpine
of windblown and semi-barren gravelly slopes and ridges.

Fig. 157   × 3/4

*Oxytropis spicata* Hook.
**Yellow Locoweed**
Fig. 158

Tufted, with one or more scapes from a stout, somewhat woody taproot. The leaves and the 1-to-2-dm-tall scape silky-hairy ; pods about 2 cm long, grey-pubescent. Dry grassy slopes. Cordilleran.

Fig. 158 × 2/3

*Oxytropis splendens* Dougl.
**Showy Locoweed**
Fig. 159

Tufted from a stout, somewhat woody branching base; leaves all basal, their numerous leaflets densely silky-hairy in whorls of three to five along the central axis; scapes 2 to 3 dm tall, terminating in a dense, elongating spike of small, dark-blue or purplish flowers; pods ovoid, densely grey-hirsute. Cordilleran species of subalpine tundra.

*Oxytropis foliolosa* Hook. is a loosely tufted, fresh green, delicate plant with slender, erect-ascending and branching stems. Flowering stalks are slightly longer than the leaves, and the inflorescence is a short raceme of from five to nine blue-violet flowers less than 1 cm long; the pods are pendulous and black-hirsute. On well-watered, calcareous gravel, commonly associated with *Dryas Hookeriana*. Arctic-alpine.

Fig. 159    × 1/2

# GERANIACEAE
## Geranium Family

*Geranium viscosissimum* Fisch. & Mey.
**Sticky Purple Cranesbill**
Fig. 160

Glandular-hirsute perennial with three- to five-lobed leaves on slender, glandular petioles, each lobe again coarsely toothed; stems up to 6 dm tall, branched above, terminating in small clusters of large, reddish purple flowers. Subalpine woodland meadows. Waterton Lakes Park.

The vernacular name is derived from the styles, which are united in a central pointed column resembling the bill of a stork or a crane; at maturity the column splits into five recoiling segments.

*Geranium Richardsonii* Fisch. & Trautv. is white-flowered and of similar habit, taller, smooth or minutely hairy, but not glandular. It is common in alpine meadows and streams.

*Geranium Bicknellii* Britt. is much smaller and diffusely branched with small, always paired, rose-coloured flowers. It is common and of somewhat weedy habit, often growing in disturbed soil by roadsides to and above timberline. All three are Cordilleran.

Fig. 160   × 3/4

## LINACEAE
## Flax Family

*Linum Lewisii* Pursh
**Wild Blue Flax**
Fig. 161

Perennial, up to 7 to 8 dm tall, often branching from the sub-woody base ; leaves alternate, linear-lanceolate, 1 to 2 cm long ; the pale blue or, rarely, white flowers in an open, few-flowered raceme ; the fruit a globular pod or capsule of five united pistils, each containing two large seeds. Dry hillsides and meadows, ascending to or above timberline. Cordilleran.

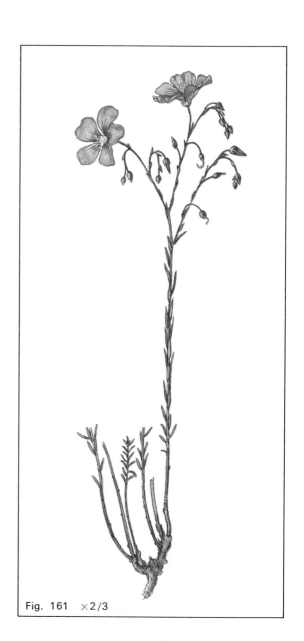

Fig. 161  ×2/3

## EMPETRACEAE
## Crowberry Family

*Empetrum nigrum* L. ssp. *hermaphroditum* (Lange) Böcher
**Black Crowberry**
Fig. 162

Depressed or spreading, freely branching, arctic-alpine, evergreen dwarf shrub with linear leaves 3 to 6 mm long, spreading and evenly distributed on the branches. The minute, bisexual flowers, two or three together in the leaf-axils, appearing early in spring as soon as the snow melts; the tiny petals crimson, and the slender stamens persisting even after the fruit is formed. Fruit edible, berry-like, juicy, black, and shiny. Not uncommon in open subalpine evergreen forest, especially on north-facing slopes, where it often forms the ground cover. Circumpolar.

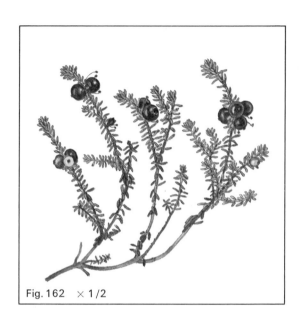

Fig. 162   × 1/2

# HYPERICACEAE
## St-John's-Wort Family

*Hypericum Scouleri* Hook.
**St-John's-Wort**
Fig. 163

Perennial herb with slender, erect stems from a thin, horizontal rootstock. The opposite oblong-elliptic leaves, with transparent dots best seen when held against a light. Flowers deep yellow, about 2 cm in diameter. Alpine slopes and meadows. Waterton Lakes Park. Cordilleran.

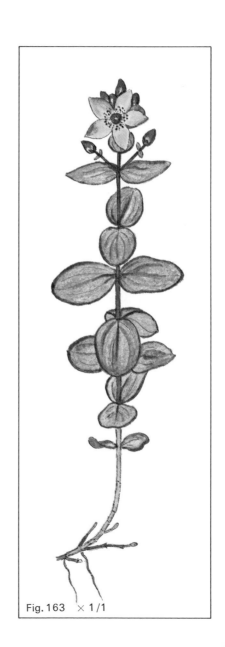

Fig. 163 $\times$ 1/1

# VIOLACEAE
## Violet Family

*Viola orbiculata* Geyer
**Yellow Violet**
Fig. 164

Dwarf species from a contracted, scaly, ascending rootstock. The leaves all basal, short-petioled, the blade roundish with toothed margin and commonly remaining green through the winter; the single pale yellow flower on a slender scape 5 to 7 cm long. Uncommon and local in damp moss, often by alpine brooks or alpine ponds. Cordilleran.

*Viola rugulosa* Greene
**Western Canada Violet**
Fig. 165

Freely branched and leafy stems up to 4 dm tall from an ascending, scaly rootstock; the basal leaves long-stalked with a heart-shaped blade, those of the stem progressively smaller and short-stalked. Flowers large and solitary from the upper leaf-axils; the petals white or pale violet with a yellow nail. Often in dense colonies in rich aspen woods. Cordilleran.

Early blue violet, *Viola adunca* J.E. Smith, is a tufted dwarf species, with a leafy branching stem 5 to 10 cm tall; the leaves long-stalked and heart-shaped, the flowers pale blue. Common on moist turfy ledges of the alpine zone. North America; subarctic.

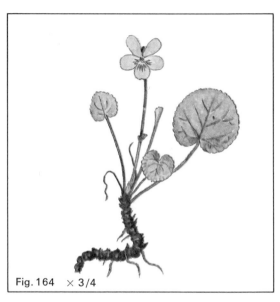

Fig. 164   × 3/4

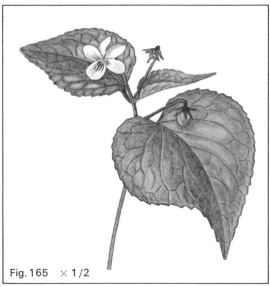

Fig. 165   × 1/2

## ELAEAGNACEAE
## Oleaster Family

*Shepherdia canadensis* (L.) Nutt.
**Canadian Buffalo-Berry**
Fig. 166

Unarmed spreading shrub, 1 to 2 m tall, with scurfy bark and opposite, leathery, broadly lanceolate leaves 2 to 5 cm long, deep green above, whereas the underside is covered by a white felt, attractively spotted by brown dots; the small, unisexual, yellowish flowers clustered in the leaf-axils; fruit small, juicy, but astringent or sour, turning scarlet when ripe. Common in not too dense woods to or slightly above timberline. North America.

Fig. 166   × 3/4

## ONAGRACEAE
## Evening Primrose Family

Represented by two genera, of which *Epilobium* (willow herb) has four petals and sepals and an elongated capsule that opens by four valves and contains rows of small seeds, each with a tuft of silky hairs at the summit. In *Circaea* the tiny, white flowers are two-parted, and the small, non-opening fruit is covered by tiny, hooked bristles.

*Epilobium anagallidifolium* Lam.
Fig. 167

Tufted dwarf species with slender, leafy runners from the base of the 5-to-15-cm-tall, S-shaped leafy stems; flowers solitary or, rarely, two or three, nodding, the petals pale pink and the very slender capsule 2 to 4 cm long and often nodding; seeds smooth. In wet moss by brooks or by the boggy edge of an alpine pond. Almost circumpolar.

*Epilobium angustifolium* L.
**Fireweed**
Fig. 168

Stems leafy, from 2 to 8 dm tall, the leaves dark green above, paler and veiny beneath. Flowers large, rose-pink, rarely white, in an elongating, leafy raceme. Common in open woods, and a ubiquitous pioneer on disturbed soil by roadsides and fire-clearings in the forest. Ascending well above timberline where it is usually smaller of stature, preferring warm, rocky slopes. Circumboreal, but not arctic.

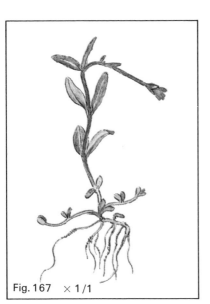

Fig. 167 × 1/1

Fig. 168 × 2/3

*Epilobium Hornemannii* Rchb.
Fig. 169

Stems 1 to 3 dm tall, in clusters from a scaly, horizontally branching
rootstock ; leaves alternate or sub-opposite, short-petioled, 2 to
4 cm long. Flowers three to six, the petals about 5 mm long, pink or
purplish ; the capsule slender, 4 to 5 cm long, the seeds minutely
tubercled. Common in damp alpine herbmats by mountain brooks.

Fig. 169 × 4/5

*Epilobium latifolium* L.
**Broad-leaved Willow-Herb**
Fig. 170

Similar to *E. angustifolium* but rarely over 4 dm tall; the leaves broader, dark green, somewhat fleshy, and often purplish-tinged when growing in the open. Flowers fewer, but larger in a short raceme. The flowers may be eaten raw as a salad, and the fleshy young leaves when cooked taste like spinach. Common and pioneering on well-watered, gravelly or sandy floodplains and river bars. Circumpolar, arctic-alpine.

Fig. 170   × 2/3

UMBELLIFERAE
**Carrot Family**

*Lomatium triternatum* (Pursh) Coult. & Rose
**Bisquit-Root**
Fig. 171

Perennial from an elongated, slender taproot; stems branching,
3 to 7 dm high, minutely hairy; the flat, narrowly oblong fruit 6 to 10
mm long, with a wing narrower than the body. Rich foothill prairie, not
truly alpine, but not uncommon in Waterton Lakes Park. Cordilleran.

Fig. 171 × 1/1

*Osmorhiza obtusa* (Coult. & Rose) Fern.
**Sweet Cicely or Antenna Plant**
Fig. 172

Perennial herb up to 6 dm tall, with a thick, aromatic root and leafy branching stems ; leaves three-parted and the leaflets variously toothed or incised ; the small, white flowers in few-flowered and few-rayed umbels ; the fruits club-shaped, obtuse or with a short-pointed tip, 1 to 1.5 cm long, their pedicels elongating and divergent in a horizontal plane, reminiscent of some TV antennas. Common in moist coniferous woods, often near an alpine brook, ascending above timberline in sheltered ravines. Cordilleran.

Fig. 172 × 2/3

*Zizia aptera* (A. Gray) Fern.
**Meadow Parsnip**
Fig. 173

Glabrous perennial, with simple or somewhat branching stem 3 to 6 dm tall from a fibrous root. Basal leaves petiolate with a heart-shaped blade, those of the stem three-parted; the small, yellow flowers in a simple cluster; fruit oblong, somewhat flattened, about 3 mm long. Rich, damp meadows, ascending to timberline north to Banff Park. Cordilleran.

Cow parsnip (*Heracleum lanatum* Michx.) is the commonest alpine representative of the Carrot Family in the Rocky Mountain parks. It has a stout, leafy stem up to 2 m tall; hairy, three-parted compound leaves up to 3 dm broad; and small, white, sweetly scented flowers in large, compound umbels. It is generally found growing among willows in sheltered hollows watered by an alpine brook. North America and eastern Asia.

Fig. 173   × 1/2

CORNACEAE
**Dogwood Family**

*Cornus canadensis* L.
**Bunchberry**
Fig. 174

Low, colony-forming perennial herb from a thin, scaly rootstock ;
stems simple, 5 to 20 cm tall ; leaves opposite, the lower small
and scaly, the upper broadly obovate in a whorl, usually of six.
Inflorescence of small, greenish, clustered flowers, subtended by
four large, white, petal-like bracts. The fruit a bright-red one- or
two-seeded drupe. Common in open coniferous woods but ascending
to or above timberline. North America and eastern Asia.

The red osier (*Cornus stolonifera*
Michx.) is a willow-like, stoloniferous
and thicket-forming shrub, 1 to 2 m tall,
with reddish purple twigs and opposite,
short-petioled, ovate-lanceolate leaves ;
the inflorescence of small white flowers
is flat-topped, and the fruit is white with
a bluish bloom. It is fairly common in
damp ravines among willows, to or
slightly above timberline. North America.

Fig. 174    × 2/3

PYROLACEAE
**Wintergreen Family**

*Chimaphila umbellata* (L.) Nutt. var. *occidentalis* (Rydb.) Blake
**Pipsissewa**
Fig. 175

Evergreen half-shrub from a long, freely branching rootstock, from which rise the 1-to-3-dm-tall leafy stems; the flowers fragrant, white or purplish, in a few-flowered cluster. Rich coniferous woods and warm alpine slopes, occasionally reaching timberline. Nearly circumboreal.

Fig. 175  × 1/1

*Moneses uniflora* (L.) Gray
**One-flowered Wintergreen**
Fig. 176

Small, delicate perennial with rounded, veiny, serrate leaves in a basal rosette, from which rises the slender scape bearing a single white flower. Its home is in shady woods, but above timberline it may be found in rich, damp leaf-mould under willows. Nearly circumboreal.

Fig. 176  × 3/2

*Pyrola bracteata* Hook.
**Bracted Wintergreen**
Fig. 177

Glabrous perennial with a thin, creeping, white rootstock ; leaves wintergreen, shiny ; the pink flowers in a spike-like terminal raceme. The fruit a dry capsule containing numerous minute, spindle-like seeds. Of Cordilleran range, its home is in rich coniferous woods and mainly in the foothills and lower valleys, but it may occasionally be found also near timberline.

Pink wintergreen (*Pyrola asarifolia* Michx.) is rather similar but has round or kidney-shaped basal leaves and larger flowers. It is not uncommon among willows in the alpine zone. North America.

Lesser wintergreen (*Pyrola minor* L.) has smaller, roundish leaves, dull green above, and small, greenish white flowers in a rather dense, spike-like raceme. Should be looked for in not too dry alpine herbmats. Circumboreal.

Arctic wintergreen (*Pyrola grandiflora* Rad.) resembles *P. bracteata*, but has fragrant, larger flowers with creamy white or pale pink petals and yellow anthers. Though circumpolar and arctic, it has been collected a few times on high mountains in Banff and Jasper Parks.

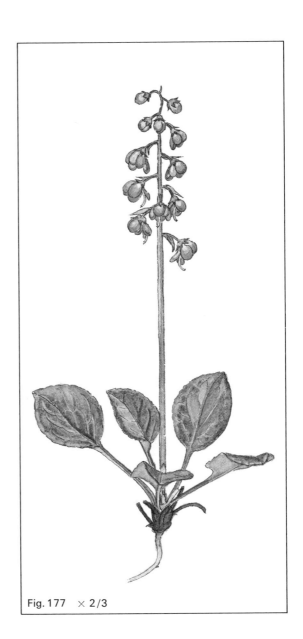

Fig. 177 × 2/3

*Pyrola secunda* L.
**One-sided Wintergreen**
Fig. 178

Stems ascending, usually several together from a branching, slender rootstock. Flowers small, bell-shaped, greenish white, in a short, one-sided raceme. Rather common, usually in herbmats or among willows, often ascending well above timberline. Circumpolar, low arctic.

Fig. 178  × 1/1

# ERICACEAE
## Heath Family

Mostly dwarf shrubs with evergreen or deciduous leaves, and perfect and regular five-parted flowers in which the corolla is often united and urn-shaped. Fruit a capsule or a berry. In the mountains, a small family composed of no less than 12 genera but with a total of only 25 species. Many are bog plants, and nearly all genera are represented in the alpine zone.

*Arctostaphylos alpina* (L.) Spreng.
**Alpine Bearberry**
Fig. 179

Mat-forming, depressed dwarf shrub with tardily deciduous, leathery, strongly net-veined leaves. The small, bell-shaped, white or pale yellow flowers appear before the new leaves are fully formed. The large, black, shiny berries are mealy and contain a few large seeds. In dry alpine tundra or on rocky ledges. Circumpolar, subarctic-alpine. Has been reported once from Jasper Park but is likely to turn up elsewhere in the parks, and always on acidic rocks.

*Arctostaphylos rubra* (Rehd. & Wilson) Fern.
**Red Bearberry**
Fig. 180

Similar to *A. alpina*, but its leaves are deciduous, larger, and thinner, turning bright red in autumn. Berries larger, bright red when ripe; although watery and insipid, they are eaten by bears and many kinds of birds. Rather common in moist and shady subalpine coniferous woods and pioneering on gravelly floodplains; always on soil derived from basic rocks.

Kinnikinnick or mealy bearberry, *Arctostaphylos Uva-Ursi* (L.) Spreng. var. *adenotricha* Fern. & McBride, is trailing or matted, with long, flat branches with rusty-red, shreddy bark, and oval, leathery, shiny evergreen leaves; flowers pale pink in small terminal racemes; the berries dull red, rather dry and mealy. Common or even ubiquitous on gravel terraces and in open coniferous woods; less common above timberline. Circumpolar.

Fig. 179  × 3/4

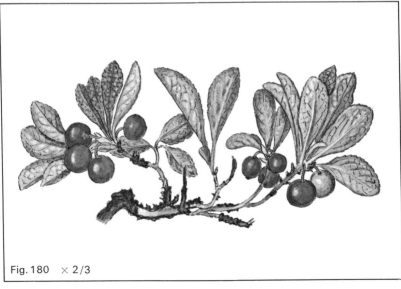

Fig. 180  × 2/3

*Cassiope Mertensiana* (Bong.) D. Don
**Mountain Heather**
Fig. 181

Similar to *C. tetragona*, from which it differs by its slenderer branches ; leaves four-ranked but not so densely crowded, and without the dorsal groove. It is rarely dominant in alpine heath but commonly grows in patches on rocky exposed slopes near and above timberline. Cordilleran.

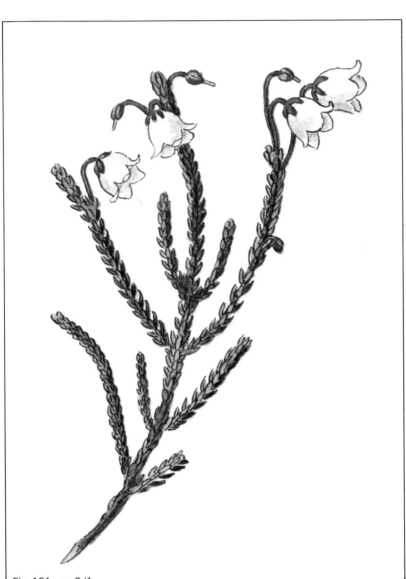

Fig. 181 × 2/1

*Cassiope tetragona* (L.) D. Don ssp. *saximontana* (Small) Porsild
**Rocky Mountain White Heather**
Fig. 182

Dwarf shrub forming dense mats near timberline on moist snowbed slopes, where it is sometimes associated with the yellow and pink mountain heath (*Phyllodoce*). Leaves four-ranked, evergreen, and scale-like, with a deep dorsal groove, and densely crowded on the slender twigs. Flowers bell-shaped, white and nodding, singly or two together from the leaf-axils near the tip of the branches. Endemic to the Rocky Mountains but closely related to the arctic and circumpolar ssp. *tetragona*, from which it differs by its smaller flowers and much shorter flowering peduncles.

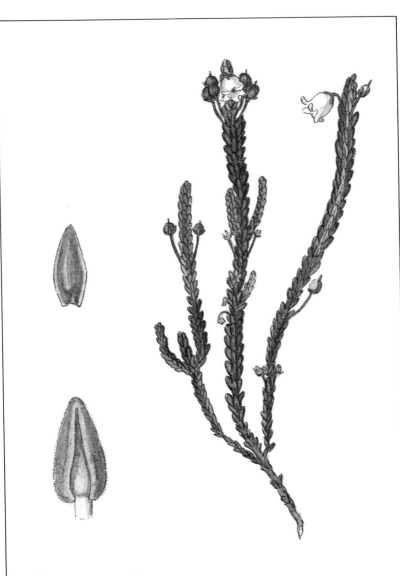

Fig. 182    × 5/3    (× 4/1)

*Kalmia polifolia* Wang. ssp. *microphylla* (Hook.) Caldor & Taylor
**Purple Laurel**
Fig. 183

Dwarf shrub 1 to 2 dm tall, with erect, somewhat branching stems; leaves lanceolate, evergreen and leathery, dark green above and glaucous beneath; the purplish, showy flowers on slender, red peduncles in a terminal cluster. Fruit a dry capsule containing numerous minute seeds. In wet places by the edge of alpine bogs.

The North American genus *Kalmia* was named by Linnaeus for one of his favourite disciples, Pehr Kalm (1717–79), one of the first professional botanists to study the floras of the northeastern United States and eastern Canada.

Labrador tea (*Ledum groenlandicum* Oeder) is a much branched aromatic shrub up to 8 dm high, but often much less, with evergreen leaves, dark green above and rusty-tomentose beneath; the small, spicy, white flowers in axillary umbels; fruit a five-valved capsule containing numerous small seeds. Subarctic, alpine.

Glandular Labrador tea (*Ledum glandulosum* Nutt.) is rather similar, but the leaves are thinner, pale green, glabrous above and glandular beneath. Common in open woods. Both North America.

Alpine azalea, *Loiseleuria procumbens* (L.) Desv., is a depressed, much branched and tufted dwarf shrub with minute, leathery, glabrous leaves and few-flowered clusters of small, pink or whitish flowers. Stony high-alpine tundra, very rare in the Rocky Mountains, south to Jasper Park. Circumpolar, arctic-alpine.

*Menziesia glabella* A. Gray is a much branched, thicket-forming shrub up to 2 m tall, with shreddy bark and 3-to-6-cm-long deciduous, oblong and serrulate leaves on glandular-hairy twigs; the small, urn-shaped, yellowish brown flowers in terminal clusters. Fruit a four-valved capsule. Common in alpine forest. Cordilleran.

*Oxycoccus microcarpus* Turcz.
**Dwarf Cranberry**
Fig. 184

Tiny, creeping dwarf shrub of alpine sphagnum bogs. The dark red, juicy, edible berries ripening in August and early September, but rarely abundant enough to provide more than a mere taste. Closely related to the eastern bog-cranberry. Circumpolar, subarctic, alpine.

Fig. 183 × 4/5

Fig. 184 × 2/3 (× 2/1)

*Phyllodoce empetriformis* (Smith) Cov.
**Purple Mountain Heath**
Fig. 185

Of similar habit and range as *P. glandulifera* but with somewhat longer leaves grooved on both sides. Flowers bell-shaped, smaller, and more numerous; the corolla pink or purplish, the sepals dark red, acute, and glabrous, as are the corollas and peduncles. Where the two species grow together a hybrid is often formed; this has the pink corollas of *P. empetriformis* and the obtuse sepals of *P. glandulifera*. Cordilleran.

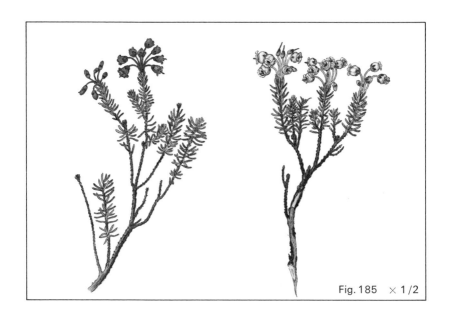

Fig. 185 × 1/2

*Phyllodoce glandulifera* (Hook.) Cov.
**Yellow Mountain Heath**
Fig. 186

Evergreen branching shrub, 1 to 3 dm high, with alternate, needle-like leaves 4 to 8 mm long and grooved beneath. Flowers urn-shaped and yellow, in terminal umbels; sepals obtuse-pointed, corollas glandular, and peduncles minutely hairy. Common near and above timberline, on moist snowbed slopes, on soils derived from acid rocks. Often associated with P. *empetriformis* and *Cassiope tetragona* ssp. *saximontana*. Cordilleran endemic reaching southeastern Alaska and mountains of the southeastern Yukon and southwestern Mackenzie District.

Fig. 186 × 3/2

*Rhododendron albiflorum* Hook.
**Rocky Mountain Rhododendron**
Fig. 187

Thicket-forming shrub rarely more than 1 m high. Leaves deciduous, pale green, oblanceolate, 3 to 7 cm long ; flowers white, 2 to 3 cm in diameter, in clusters of two or three from the old wood below the new terminal shoots. Mainly along the Continental Divide, in cool, damp openings of Engelmann-spruce and pine forest, and always on acid soil ; in sheltered gullies it may occasionally ascend above timberline. Cordilleran.

Fig. 187  × 1/1

*Rhododendron lapponicum* (L.) Wahlenb.
**Lapland Rosebay**
Fig. 188

Erect or depressed, much branched shrub, rarely more than 3 dm high; leaves evergreen, leathery, dark green above, the underside with rust-coloured, scaly hairs; its purplish, faintly scented flowers opening soon after the snow melts. Although described from Scandinavia, where it is restricted to two isolated areas in Norway, the main range of the Lapland rosebay is in alpine and subarctic North America and eastern Siberia. It was discovered only recently in the Rocky Mountains, where, thus far, it is known only from two mountains in the eastern foothill ranges east of Jasper Park. Its preferred habitat is in open stony or gravelly tundra, always on non-acid rocks.

Fig. 188   × 1/1

*Vaccinium scoparium* Leiberg
**Pink-fruited Grouse-Berry**
Fig. 189

Dwarf shrub, 1 to 2 dm high, which, unlike the species listed below, has angular branches that remain green for several years ; leaves deciduous, about 1 cm long, bright green on both sides, with finely serrated margins. Flowers solitary in the leaf-axils, small, urn-shaped, pale pink ; the berries bright coral-red, only 5 mm in diameter, tart but edible. A timberline species of moist alpine slopes, where it often forms the ground cover. Central Rocky Mountains.

Tall blueberry (*Vaccinium membrana-ceum* Dougl.) is an erect shrub, 1 m high or more, with lanceolate, thin leaves up to 5 cm long, and large, blue berries. It is not truly alpine but ascends to slightly beyond timberline on sheltered, south-facing slopes.

Dwarf blueberry (*Vaccinium caespito-sum* Michx.) is much branched, nearly always prostrate, with small, distinctly serrate leaves and small, blue, edible berries. It is not uncommon in open subalpine forest and is occasional on sheltered slopes beyond timberline. Labrador and southeastern Alaska.

The circumpolar arctic bog blueberry (*Vaccinium uliginosum*) is of similar habit, but the leaves are entire and prominently veined beneath ; its berries are blue with a greyish bloom and are very sweet and juicy. It has been collected a few times on stony ledges far above timberline in Jasper Park, where it was associated with other arctic species.

Fig. 189   × 1/1

*Vaccinium Vitis-Idaea* L. var. *minus* Lodd
**Mountain Cranberry**
Fig. 190

Low, creeping dwarf shrub, common in open alpine spruce and fir forest, and occasional among willows above timberline. Its shiny, dark green, leathery leaves remain green through the winter; flowers white or pink, in small, nodding terminal clusters. The tart, dark red, shiny berries ripen but remain on the vines throughout the winter, when their flavour improves with freezing; when gathered in the autumn they may be kept frozen until used. In Norway and Sweden, "lingon" berries are greatly in demand for making the justly famous Scandinavian cranberry sauce and are excellent also for pies and jellies. Circumpolar, subarctic, alpine.

Fig. 190  × 1/1

# PRIMULACEAE
## Primrose Family

Herbs with simple and mostly opposite or whorled leaves. Flowers perfect ; calyx and corolla more or less united, the stamens inserted in the corolla tube ; the ovary superior, one-celled. Fruit a capsule ; those dealt with here opening from the top with five valves.

A small family, in the mountains represented by four genera and less than a dozen species, of which only a few are alpine.

*Androsace Chamaejasme* Host
**Rock-Jasmine**
Fig. 191

Loosely tufted perennial with a branching horizontal stem, from the nodes of which rise small rosettes of crowded, linear, stiffly ciliated leaves about 5 mm long. Flowers sweet-scented, small and umbellate, on a short, erect scape, the petals white or sometimes pink, with a yellow eye. Common on rocky calcareous ledges or screes. Eastern Asia and North America ; arctic-alpine.

*Androsace septentrionalis* L.
Fig. 192

Dwarf annual, greatly varying in size from a few cm to 20 cm tall according to habitat and condition of soil. Leaves in a small basal rosette, from which rise one to several flowering scapes, each terminating in an umbel of small, white flowers. Fairly common in damp shady places, often pioneering on disturbed soil far beyond timberline. Circumpolar, arctic-alpine.

Fig. 191   × 1/2

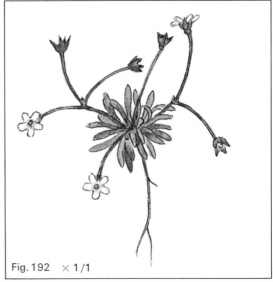

Fig. 192   × 1/1

*Dodecatheon pauciflorum* (Dur.) Greene
**Shooting Star**
Fig. 193

Perennial, 1 to 4 dm tall, with clusters of nodding, purple flowers. As the seeds mature, the peduncles straighten so that the cylindrical capsules become stiffly erect. In wet mossy places, among willows, often by the outflow from cold mineral springs. Cordilleran.

*Primula mistassinica* Michx.
**Bird's-Eye Primrose**
Fig. 194

Perennial from a rosette of small, minutely toothed, green, oval leaves. Flowering scapes from 10 to 15 cm tall. Commonly in small colonies around the mother plant ; in wet calcareous soil by pond margins or in wet meadows.

Mealy primrose (*Primula incana* Jones) is stouter and taller ; the calyx, the floral bracts, and also the underside of the sinuate-margined, oblong rosette leaves are conspicuously white-mealy. Prefers damp, alkaline meadows such as are often found near the outflow of mineral springs.

*Primula egaliksensis* Wormskj., first discovered at Igaliko in South Greenland, is smaller than *P. mistassinica ;* the leaves are oblanceolate, thin, entire-margined, green ; the corolla is white with deeply cleft lobes. In mossy places, often along alpine brooks. All three are native of North America.

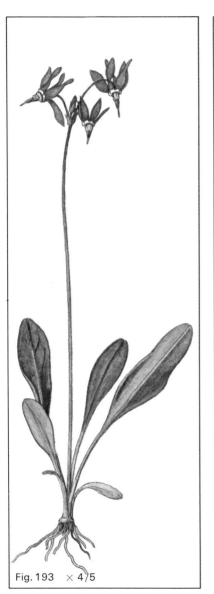

Fig. 193 × 4/5

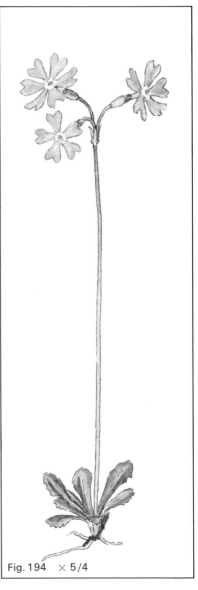

Fig. 194 × 5/4

# GENTIANACEAE
## Gentian Family

Whereas alpine meadows of the European Alps and the Pyrenees are justly famed for their great variety of showy gentians, the genus is not so well represented in the northern Rocky Mountains, where, moreover, most of the species found are small-flowered and not so showy.

*Gentiana affinis* Griseb.
## Prairie Gentian
Fig. 195

Late-flowering perennial from a scaly rootstock; stems leafy, usually several together, 1 to 3 dm tall, with a terminal cluster of two or three pairs of short-pedicelled flowers. The corolla purplish blue, 2 to 3 cm long. Not uncommon locally on rocky calcareous slopes but rarely reaching timberline. Southern British Columbia east to southern Manitoba.

*Gentiana Forwoodii* A. Gray is rather similar, but the flowering pedicels are shorter, as are the lobes of the calyx. Of more southern range. Waterton Lakes Park.

Blue green gentian (*Gentiana glauca* Pall.) also perennial, but with stems only 5 to 12 cm high, of matted habit and arctic amphi-Beringian range, is not uncommon on alpine ledges in Jasper and Banff Parks; its leaves mostly basal; its smaller, greenish blue flowers in a few-flowered terminal cluster.

*Gentiana arctophila* Griseb.
## Felwort
Fig. 196

This and the rather similar *Gentiana propinqua* Richards. are glabrous annuals and mostly gregarious species with a purplish, simple or branched stem, 5 to 25 cm tall from a rosette of oblanceolate entire leaves. In exposed alpine situations the flowering stem is usually unbranched and only a few cm high, whereas at lower elevations it may be richly branched from the base, with up to a dozen opposite flowers on slender pedicels from the upper leaf-axils. The terminal flower is always largest. Corollas pale violet, 10 to 15 mm long. Northwestern Arctic and North America.

*Gentiana acuta* Michx. is rather similar but smaller-flowered, and the throat of the corolla is always fringed. Labrador to southwestern Alaska.

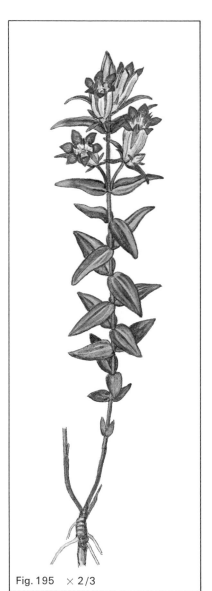

Fig. 195 × 2/3

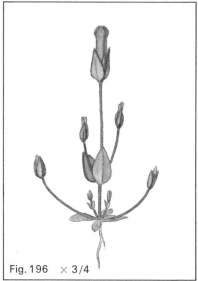

Fig. 196 × 3/4

*Gentiana Macounii* Th. Holm
**Macoun's Gentian**
Fig. 197

Annual or biennial with a small rosette of spatulate or lanceolate leaves and a stiff angular stem, 1 to 3 dm tall; with a single terminal flower or, in vigorous specimens, one or several smaller flowers on branches from the lower leaf-axils. The corolla is deep blue, 1.5 to 3 cm long, and the lobes are fringed. Common locally in wet calcareous meadows, often by the outflow of mineral springs. Cordilleran.

*Gentiana prostrata* Haenke
Fig. 198

Tiny annual or biennial, often but a few cm high, branching from the base, with tiny, pale green leaves only a few mm long, and a solitary terminal flower. The sky-blue corolla opens only in bright sunshine but closes within seconds when a cloud passes before the sun. Despite its tiny size, it is one of the prettiest of the alpine gentians and not uncommon in alpine tundra or on rocky ledges well above timberline. Western North America and the mountains of Eurasia.

Fig. 197   × 3/4

Fig. 198   × 3/4

# POLEMONIACEAE
## Phlox Family

*Polemonium pulcherrimum* Hook.
**Jacob's Ladder**
Fig. 199

Perennial, viscid-puberulent herb with reddish purple flowering stems 3 dm high, simple or branched above ; leaves mainly basal, pinnate, with ten to fifteen pairs of ovate or rounded leaflets. Flowers in a terminal cluster ; corolla wheel-shaped, about 1 cm in diameter, purple with a yellow centre. Fruit a three-celled capsule. Common locally in Waterton and Banff Parks, mainly in calcareous alpine meadows and by brooks. Northwestern North America.

Tall Jacob's ladder (*Polemonium acutiflorum* Willd.) has stems usually solitary and 3 to 7 dm tall ; leaves non-glandular with fewer and lanceolate leaflets ; the corollas bell-shaped, commonly 2 cm in diameter, pale blue or purplish, and the lobes always ciliate-margined. Arctic-alpine. Jasper Park.

Skunkweed (*Polemonium viscosum* Nutt.) is much smaller, strongly viscid-puberulent, with large, minutely pubescent corollas ; its leaves are short with numerous roundish leaflets, whorled on the leaf-stalk. Mainly in Waterton Lakes Park.

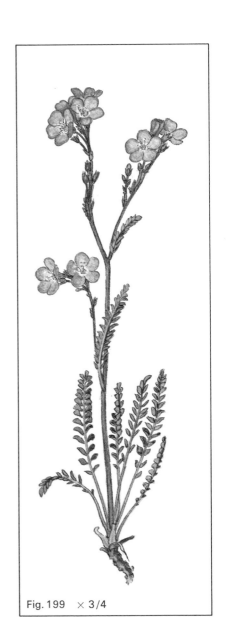

Fig. 199   × 3/4

# HYDROPHYLLACEAE
## Waterleaf Family

*Phacelia sericea* (Grah.) A. Gray
**Scorpion-Weed**
Fig. 200

Perennial from ascending and branching rootstock, from which rise
the one to several stiffly erect, 1-to-3-dm-tall, leafy stems. Leaves
oblong, pinnately divided, green above and appressed-silky beneath.
Inflorescence spike-like of rather large, purple flowers. Not
uncommon, especially on sliderock above timberline. Cordilleran.

*Phacelia Franklinii* Gray is a biennial or short-lived perennial of boreal woodland range, but is not alpine ; it is of weedy habit and often pioneers on disturbed soil ; collected a few times in the eastern ranges, but outside the Rocky Mountain parks.

Fig. 200 × 3/4

*Romanzoffia sitchensis* Bong.
Fig. 201

Low perennial from a scaly or bulbiferous rootstock. Leaves with long, slender petioles that are conspicuously dilated at the base, and with a kidney-shaped, five- to seven-lobed blade; the flowering stem few-leaved, 10 to 15 cm tall, bearing one to several flowers; corolla white with a yellow throat. Fruit a two-valved capsule containing numerous seeds. A coastal species of wet alpine situations, in the parks known only from a single station in Banff Park.

Fig. 201  × 2/3

BORAGINACEAE
**Borage Family**

*Mertensia paniculata* (Ait.) G. Don
**Lungwort**
Fig. 202

Stems mostly several, 3 to 6 dm tall from a branching, somewhat woody base; basal leaves lanceolate, hairy on both sides, on slender, winged petioles, leaves of the stems stalkless; flowers in drooping clusters, the corolla tubular and bell-shaped, pink in bud but bright blue when fully expanded; the long, slender style slightly protruding. Fruits four-angled dry nutlets. Common by alpine brooks and in damp willow or alder thickets. North America.

Fig. 202  × 4/5

*Myosotis alpestris* F. W. Schm. ssp. *asiatica* Vestergr.
**Alpine Forget-me-not**
Fig. 203

Tufted, erect, tomentose perennial herb with oblong, conspicuously petioled basal leaves and sessile stem-leaves; stems mostly 1 to 2 dm tall; flowers very fragrant, first congested, elongating into one-sided racemes; the corolla, 4 to 6 mm in diameter, bright blue with a yellow centre; the nutlets smooth and shiny. Common and often in dense clusters, mostly above timberline. Northwestern America and eastern Asia.

Fig. 203  × 1/1

## LABIATAE
## Mint Family

*Monarda fistulosa* L. var *menthaefolia* (Grah.) Fern.
**Horsemint**
Fig. 204

Slender, opposite-leaved, aromatic perennial from a slender, creeping rootstock; flowering stems commonly 2 to 4 dm tall, four-angled and leafy, the leaves toothed and the lowermost short-petioled. Flowers in a showy terminal cluster; the two-lipped corolla 2 to 2.5 cm long, lilac. Fruit of four nutlets. Dry, sunny slopes of the eastern foothills, mainly in Waterton Park but local north to Kananaskis, east of Banff Park.

*Prunella vulgaris* L. var. *lanceolata* (Bart.) Fern.
**Self-heal**
Fig. 205

Low perennial herb from a branching rootstock; the flowers irregular in a short, leafy, terminal spike; the corolla two-lipped, the upper lip arched, the lower three-parted. In moist places often by alpine brooks. North America.

Fig. 204 × 2/3

Fig. 205 × 1/2

# SCROPHULARIACEAE
## Figwort Family

Chiefly perennial herbs, with opposite or alternate leaves and axillary, racemose or spicate inflorescence of mostly irregular flowers, and two-locular, many-seeded capsules; several at least partly parasitic on the roots of other plants.

In the parks represented by 12 genera, of which 5, with about 40 species, are alpine.

*Castilleja miniata* Dougl.
**Indian Paintbrush**
Fig. 206

This is easily the showiest of the Rocky Mountain *Castilleja*. Its preferred habitat is on south-facing, well-drained slopes or rocky ledges, where it often forms large clumps from a scaly, much branched rootstock. In common with several other members of the genus, the tips of the leafy bracts that subtend the individual flowers in inflorescence are as highly coloured as are the corollas.

Sometimes associated with *Castilleja miniata*, especially on moister habitats, are other species, some with bright yellow flowers, some with pink or flesh-coloured (*C. rhexifolia*) flowers.

*Castilleja* is a large, taxonomically difficult, mainly North American genus; most species are root-parasites, and many are endemic to the Rocky Mountain region.

Fig. 206   × 3/4

*Castilleja occidentalis* Torr.
Fig. 207

Stems mostly solitary, rarely more than 25 cm high, from a short ascending rootstock ; bracts hairy, somewhat glandular, yellow in life, drying dark green ; corollas lemon-yellow in life, turning black in drying. Common in rather dry high-alpine tundra. Cordilleran.

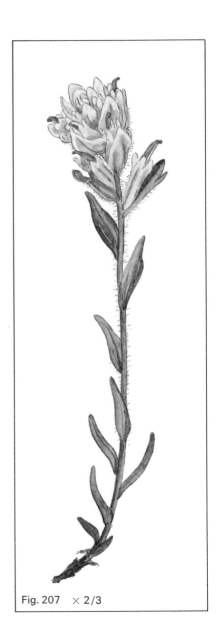

Fig. 207   × 2/3

*Mimulus guttatus* DC.
**Yellow Monkey-Flower**
Fig. 208

Annual or short-lived, delicate perennial up to 3 dm tall, with large, yellow flowers. Common locally in moist peaty or gravelly places, often by the edge of mineral springs. Its main range is along the moist coast ranges from California northward to Alaska ; in Canada with a few often widely separated stations in the interior, where it is mainly restricted to springs or local areas that, owing to topographic features, enjoy heavy precipitation.

Fig. 208   × 1/1

*Mimulus Lewisii* Pursh
**Red Monkey-Flower**
Fig. 209

In Waterton Lakes Park one of the showiest and most spectacular
alpines, which unfortunately barely enters Alberta. It is perennial,
and the stems, leaves, and flowering peduncles are glandular-hairy ;
its favorite habitat is by ice-cold mountain streams, where it often
grows in solid masses in places reached by the spray of the cascading
brooks. Cordilleran endemic, which through the mountains of
British Columbia barely reaches southeastern Alaska.

Fig. 209   × 1/1

*Pedicularis contorta* Benth.
**Lousewort**
Fig. 210

Flowering stems leafy, one to several together from a short, branching rootstock; the flowers bright creamy-white in an 8-to-12-cm-long raceme. Not uncommon on alpine herbmat slopes, usually in solitary clumps, which from a distance resemble lighted candles.

Bracted lousewort (*Pedicularis bracteosa* Benth.) is up to 1 m tall, with lanceolate, crenulate leaves and an elongated, leafy-bracted spike of pinkish yellow flowers subtended by a whorl of leafy bracts. It grows on turfy slopes, near alpine brooks or seepages, or among willows and scrub conifers, near or above timberline. Cordilleran, as is *P. contorta*.

*Pedicularis Oederi* Vahl is much smaller, often less than 20 cm tall, with a densely woolly spike of yellow and purple flowers. It is always rare and local, and grows in damp alpine tundra.

Woolly lousewort (*Pedicularis lanata* Cham. & Schlecht.) is very showy, with a densely woolly spike of pink, sweet-scented flowers, much elongated in fruit. The strong taproot is bright yellow.

Arctic lousewort (*Pedicularis arctica* R. Br.) is rather similar but differs from *P. lanata* by the more arching upper lip of its corolla, which has a small, sharp tooth on each side of the hood, and by its pale, almost white taproot.

The last three species represent members of a now widely separated and isolated arctic element of the Rocky Mountain flora and are restricted to the high-alpine zone.

Few-flowered lousewort (*Pedicularis capitata* Adams) is a dwarf species with a slender, horizontally creeping rootstock from which rise the 5-to-15-cm-tall scapes, each terminating in a capitate, two- to four-flowered head, subtended by a cluster of leafy bracts; the flowers are creamy-yellow and scentless, the basal leaves pinnate, the blade oblong, and the pinnae coarsely serrate with hard, white incrustations along the margins. It is common in alpine herbmats, but mainly in calcareous soil. Circumpolar, arctic-alpine.

Fig. 210 × 2/3

*Pedicularis groenlandica* Oeder
**Elephant's Head**
Fig. 211

Essentially glabrous perennial from a weak and freely branched tap-root, common locally in rich, subalpine, and rather moist calcareous meadows or by seepages from mineral springs, where it often forms large colonies. The elephant's head is at once distinguished from other members of the genus in the parks by its up to 25-cm-long, slender spike of reddish purple flowers. Its vernacular name alludes to the shape of its flower, which in profile bears a striking likeness to that of an elephant's head with its trunk raised high — the "trunk" being the greatly prolonged, tubular, 1.5-cm-long tip of the upper lip of the corolla that encloses the long style, and the reflexed lateral lobes of the lower lip simulating the ear lobes of the "elephant". Subarctic-alpine, from western Greenland to Alaska.

Fig. 211 × 2/3 (× 3/1)

*Penstemon fruticosus* (Pursh) Greene
**Shrubby Beard-Tongue**
Fig. 212

A decumbent dwarf shrub with trailing, leafy stems, somewhat leathery, wintergreen leaves, and a terminal cluster of large, purplish blue flowers. Common locally on rocky alpine ledges and endemic to the central Rockies. The genus *Penstemon* is almost entirely North American, and in the Rocky Mountains alone is represented by well over one hundred species, of which about a dozen occur in the Rocky Mountain parks.

Fig. 212   × 1/2

*Penstemon Lyallii* A. Gray
**Lyall's Beard-Tongue**
Fig. 213

Essentially glabrous perennial from a somewhat woody base. With its erect leafy stem, sometimes 6 dm high, it is the tallest member of the genus within the Rocky Mountain parks, where, together with *Penstemon acuminatus* Dougl. and *P. albidus* Nutt., it is found only in Waterton Lakes Park; the light, blue-flowered *P. albertinus* Greene, however, has been collected once in Banff Park.

Fig. 213  × 1/1

*Penstemon procerus* Dougl.
## Blue Beard-Tongue
Fig. 214

Erect, glabrous perennial, with slender stems 2 to 3 dm tall from an ascending, somewhat woody rootstock; the small, bright-blue flowers whorled in an interrupted spike. Common in rather dry subalpine grassland, only occasional at timberline.

Yellow beard-tongue (*Penstemon confertus* Dougl.) is similar in habit but has bright yellow flowers; not uncommon in alpine herbmats, and in Banff Park may be seen well above timberline.

*Veronica alpina* L.
## Alpine Speedwell
Fig. 215

This is the only common member of the genus in alpine herbmats and on moist rocky ledges. The tiny, deep-blue flowers are first clustered but soon elongate into an open spike-like raceme in the var. *alterniflora* Fern., in which the capsules are smooth, whereas in var. *Wormskjoldii* the capsules are glandular-hairy and the inflorescence remains short and dense.

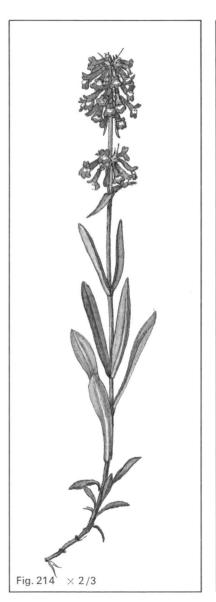

Fig. 214  × 2/3

Fig. 215  × 2/3  (× 3/1)

## LENTIBULARIACEAE
## Bladderwort Family

Three species of Bladderwort (*Utricularia*) have been recorded
from ponds and quiet lakes in Banff Park, but never in the alpine
zone. The bladderworts are submersed aquatic plants with emergent
yellow flowers and finely divided leaves ; some of these divisions are
green, and some are pale, transparent, bladder-like traps ; the
entrance to the "trap" is narrowed by a collar of inward-pointed hairs,
which allows tiny aquatic animals to enter but prevents their escape.
The trapped animals eventually die and decompose, thereby
providing a source of nitrogenous nutrients for the plant.

*Pinguicula vulgaris* L.
**Butterwort**
Fig. 216

Common locally on moist calcareous soil, by cold springs or
seepages and on hummocks in wet meadows ; mainly in mountain
valleys and rarely ascending to timberline. The upper surface of its
fleshy leaves is covered by minute, sticky glands that trap and digest
small insects, thereby supplying the plant with nitrogen and other
nutrients. Circumpolar, subarctic-alpine.

Fig. 216  × 1/1

# RUBIACEAE
**Madder Family**

*Galium boreale* L.
**Northern Bedstraw**
Fig. 217

Perennial herb with clustered, simple or branched, leafy stems up to 7 dm tall from a branching sub-woody base; leaves sessile, linear or linear-lanceolate, in whorls of four; the small, regular, fragrant flowers in terminal, many-flowered compound cymes; the corollas white, four-parted; the fruit two-parted, at maturity splitting into separate bristly achenes. Common on open, dry hillsides. Circumpolar.

Sweet-scented bedstraw (*Galium triflorum* Michx.) has weak, strongly bristly, freely forking stems and thin, deep-green leaves in whorls of six. Though a plant of damp, rich woodlands, it ascends to or near timberline, where it may be found on leaf-mould under alders. Very fragrant in drying and for this reason was formerly mixed with mattress straw to "sweeten" bedroom odours.

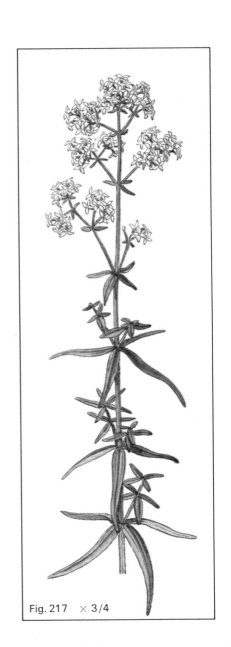

Fig. 217 × 3/4

## CAPRIFOLIACEAE
**Honeysuckle Family**

*Linnaea borealis* L. var. *americana* (Forbes) Rehd.
**Twin-Flower**
Fig. 218

Although the home of this circumboreal, elegant, sweet-scented evergreen is in open, cool, mossy coniferous woods, it quite often ascends to and even beyond timberline. Its tiny, dry fruits are sticky from tiny, hooked bristles and readily become attached to the fur of animals or the feathers of woodland birds. The genus *Linnaea* was named for the Swedish botanist, Linnaeus, the father of modern taxonomy, with whom this pretty little plant was a favourite.

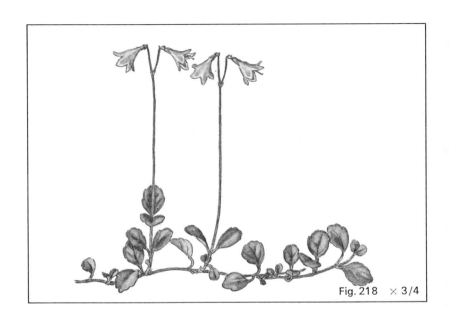

Fig. 218   × 3/4

*Lonicera involucrata* Banks
**Bracted Honeysuckle**
Fig. 219

A low, twining or reclining shrub, common in damp thickets and along subalpine streams and, with twin flower (*Linnaea*) and high-bush cranberry (*Viburnum edule*), the only members of the Honey-suckle Family that, in the parks, regularly ascends to or slightly above timberline. It is showiest in fruit, when its large, black, shiny twin-berries are loosely enclosed in a "cup", formed by petal-like, dark red bracts. North America.

Fig. 219 × 4/5

*Viburnum edule* (Michx.) Raf.
**High-Bush Cranberry**
Fig. 220

A handsome flowering shrub of moist woodland situations, where it commonly grows erect and up to 2 m tall, but near timberline is much lower. Its tart, bright red fruits are edible and formerly were gathered and dried by northern Indian tribes to sweeten their pemmican. The fruits remain on the branches through the winter and are even better flavoured after the first frost. When the large seeds are strained out, a beautifully coloured and deliciously flavoured jelly may be made from the juice. North America.

Fig. 220   × 2/3

## VALERIANACEAE
## Valerian Family

*Valeriana sitchensis* Bong.
**Valerian**
Fig. 221

Essentially smooth herb with opposite, pinnately divided leaves ; flowering stems 4 to 8 dm tall, solitary or few together from a somewhat fleshy rootstock ; the numerous regular, small, white or pinkish flowers in a hemispherical terminal head. The fruit a dry achene equipped with feathery bristles, by which it readily becomes airborne. Cordilleran, alpine.

Northern valerian (*Valeriana septentrionalis* Rydb.) is a slenderer plant in which the basal leaves are entire, spatulate, or elliptic in outline. Mainly in foothill bogs. Cordilleran.

All members of this genus tend to be strongly aromatic ; this is most noticeable in autumn after the first night-frosts, when the odour emitted by *Valeriana sitchensis* may become rather oppressive.

Fig. 221   × 2/3

# CAMPANULACEAE
## Bluebell Family

*Campanula lasiocarpa* Cham.
## Alpine Harebell
Fig. 222

Glabrous perennial from a spindly taproot; stem rarely more than 10 cm tall, terminating in a single erect, bright blue flower that even on dwarf specimens may be as much as 3 cm long. Western arctic species of alpine stony tundra or screes; in this area collected only a few times. Amphi-Beringian.

*Campanula Parryi* A. Gray is somewhat taller; its basal leaves are spatulate, dentate or entire, glabrous, the upper linear; the single erect flower narrowly funnelform, cleft to the middle, and its sepals glabrous, awl-shaped, and entire, not toothed or hirsute as in the rather similar *Campanula lasiocarpa*. A rare Cordilleran species not heretofore recognized from Canada, where it has been collected at Carthew Lake in Waterton Lakes Park and in southern British Columbia. It should be looked for elsewhere in the mountains of southern Alberta and British Columbia.

*Campanula rotundifolia* L.
## Common Harebell
Fig. 223

Glabrous perennial with 1-to-4-dm-high stems; basal leaves long-petioled, the blade oval or heart-shaped, but often wilted and gone at time of flowering; stem-leaves linear and sessile and the flowers bright blue, nodding, 2 to 3 cm long, usually solitary, on a long, slender peduncle. The only common bluebell of the parks, where it grows in open sandy or gravelly places; ascending above timberline. Circumpolar, arctic-alpine.

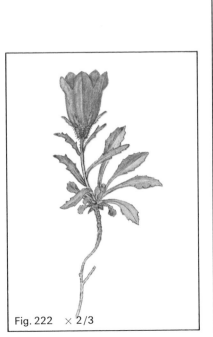

Fig. 222　× 2/3

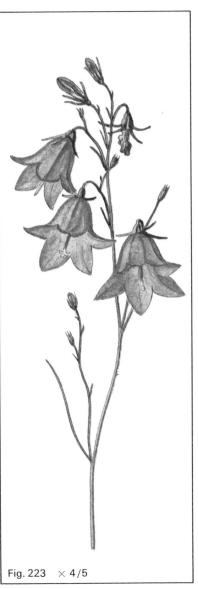

Fig. 223　× 4/5

*Campanula uniflora* L.
**Dwarf Harebell**
Fig. 224

Glabrous, with one to several erect or ascending leafy stems, 5 to 15 cm tall from a fleshy simple or branching taproot. The single small, deep-blue flower at first nodding, but as the hairy capsule ripens, becoming stiffly erect. Circumpolar arctic species exceedingly rare and local in the area, where it should be looked for above timberline in turfy places on basic and well-drained soils.

Fig. 224   × 3/4

# LOBELIACEAE
## Lobelia Family

*Lobelia Kalmii* L.
**Kalm's Lobelia**
Fig. 225

Biennial ; stems mostly simple, from 5 to 25 cm high, from a leafy rosette formed the first year ; the pale blue flowers in an open raceme. Its favorite habitat is on wet calcareous mud, frequently by the outflow from a cold mineral spring, where it is often conspicuous by its densely massed growth. *Lobelia Kalmii* was named by Linnaeus for its discoverer, Pehr Kalm, his favourite pupil. Boreal North America.

Fig. 225 × 2/3

# COMPOSITAE
## Composite Family

A very large and complex family. In the Rocky Mountains mainly represented by herbaceous species, although several with somewhat woody base. Flowers small, aggregated on a flat, concave or convex common receptacle into a closed head, resembling a single often large flower. The individual flowers are all alike, or those of the centre are tubular and different from those of the margin. The flowering head is said to be *discoid* when the corollas of all flowers are tubular; *ligulate* when the corollas are irregular, one-sided, and strap-like; and *radiate* when the central flowers are tubular and discoid and the radial or rayflowers strap-like (ligulate). Calyx lacking or converted into persistent scales, capillary bristles, or hairs (pappus) that serve in the dispersal of the mostly elongated, dry, nut-like fruits (achenes) by wind or by their ability to adhere to the fur of animals. Stamens five, usually united into a tube, through which the simple, usually two-cleft style protrudes.

In the Rocky Mountain parks represented by 32 genera, of which *Solidago, Aster, Erigeron, Antennaria, Artemisia, Arnica*, and *Senecio* account for 140 of the total of 205 species. A good many members of the family are prairie or grassland species, which in the parks are confined mainly to east-facing valleys; a comparatively small number are true alpines.

KEY TO THE MORE EASILY RECOGNIZED GENERA OF
ROCKY MOUNTAIN COMPOSITAE

a  Corollas all ligulate; plants with milky sap or juice

   b  Plants scapose, the leaves all basal

      c  Achenes spinulose, corollas yellow — *Taraxacum*, p. 430

      c  Achenes smooth, corollas orange-reddish — *Agoseris*, p. 382

   b  Plants with leafy stems

      d  Pappus brownish; root fibrous — *Hieracium*, p. 418

      d  Pappus white; roots simple or branching — *Crepis*, p. 408

a  Heads discoid; central flowers bisexual, all tubular and only the marginal (when present) ligulate or strap-like, pistillate or neutral; plants with watery sap or juice

      e  Heads of only tubular flowers

         f  Receptacle densely bristly — *Saussurea*, p. 422

         f  Receptacle naked

            g  Pappus of capillary bristles

               h  Involucral bracts (phyllaries) thin and more or less translucent; plant white or greenish grey, tomentose — *Antennaria*, p. 386

    h  Involucral bracts firm or at most with
       translucent margins

      i  Leaves all basal; flowering stem
         pale and scaly; flowers whitish,
         scented                        *Petasites*, p. 420
      i  Stem-leaves present, flowers
         yellow, unscented            *Senecio*, p. 424

   g  Pappus of scales or chaffy bristles

      j  Rayflowers purplish blue or
         yellow, leaves entire         *Townsendia*, p. 432
      j  Rayflowers white or pink, leaves
         pinnately dissected        *Achillea*, p. 382

e  Heads of tubular and ligulate flowers; pappus
   of capillary bristles

        k  Rays or ligulate flowers yellow

           l  Leaves opposite        *Arnica*, p. 394
           l  Leaves alternate

             m Heads solitary up to
                6 cm in diameter     *Gaillardia*, p. 416
             m Heads smaller

                n  Pappus double    *Chrysopsis*, p. 406
                n  Pappus simple

                   o  Involucral bracts in
                      a single row     *Senecio*, p. 424
                   o  Involucral bracts in
                      several rows     *Solidago*, p. 428

        k  Rays or ligulate flowers not
          yellow

                   p  Leaves ap-
                      pearing after
                      flowering      *Petasites*, p. 420
                   p  Leaves ap-
                      pearing before
                      flowering

                     q  Heads on
                        leafy stems    *Aster*, p. 402
                     q  Heads on
                        naked or
                        few-leaved
                        peduncles     *Erigeron*, p. 410

*Achillea nigrescens* (E. Mey.) Rydb.
**Yarrow or Milfoil**
Fig. 226

Aromatic, somewhat villous perennial with alternate, double-pinnate leaves from a horizontally creeping rootstock ; stems 2 to 4 dm tall with a terminal flat-topped cluster of small heads ; involucral bracts straw-coloured with black margins ; rayflowers few, white or pink, the disk flowers more numerous, with yellow or straw-coloured corollas ; the achenes smooth without a pappus. Boreal North America.

Woolly milfoil (*Achillea lanulosa* Nutt.) is somewhat similar but has densely villous stems and up to 10-cm-long pinnatifid leaves ; the involucral bracts are light brown with paler margins. Arctic-alpine, commonly growing in sandy or gravelly places.

*Agoseris aurantiaca* (Hook.) Greene
**False Dandelion**
Fig. 227

Perennial, up to 5-to-6-dm-tall, scapose herb from a strong, ascending rootstock and mostly entire, or shallowly toothed, elongated basal leaves ; head solitary, the flowers all ligulate and mostly reddish orange ; the achenes oblong with a white pappus. Rocky Mountain foothill or alpine meadows, ascending to or slightly above timberline.

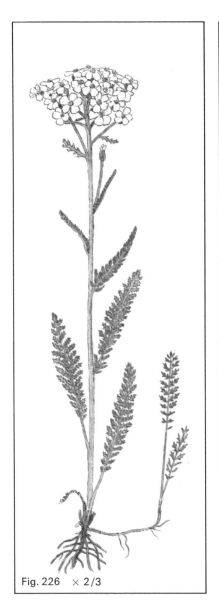

Fig. 226 × 2/3

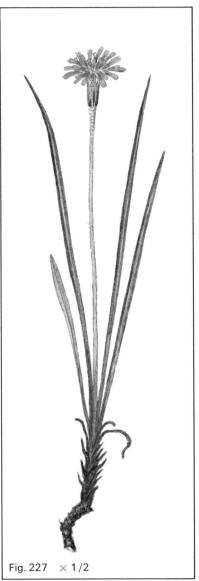

Fig. 227 × 1/2

*Agoseris glauca* (Pursh) Raf.
Fig. 228

Similar to *A. aurantiaca*, but leaves are oblanceolate and entire-margined and scapes rarely more than 2 to 3 dm tall ; head of yellow flowers, which usually turn pink in drying. Rocky Mountains.

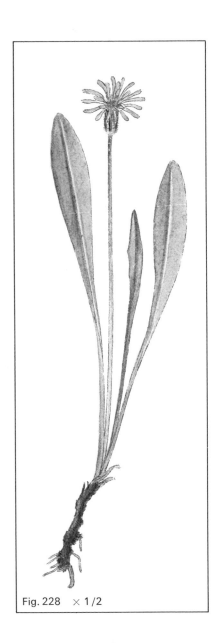

Fig. 228 × 1/2

*Antennaria*
**Everlasting**

Dioecious, woolly or silky, mat-forming or, less commonly, tufted perennial herbs. Leaves alternate, the basal ones often in a rosette ; those of the matted species small, often strap-like or oblanceolate, whereas in the tufted species they are longer and often prominently three- to five-nerved. Heads discoid and small, commonly three to seven in a compact cluster, rarely solitary ; in some species the male plant is rare or unknown when seeds are formed without fertilization. Flowers of the female plant with filiform, tubular corollas enclosed by three or more rows of translucent white- , grey- , or pink-tipped involucral bracts. Achenes with a pappus of fine white or pale grey bristles ; pappus bristles of the male plant club-shaped.

In North America this is a large and taxonomically difficult genus. About a dozen species, including some of the most interesting ones, are confined to the alpine zone.

*Antennaria lanata* Hook.
**Woolly Everlasting**
Fig. 229

Tufted from a stout, ascending rootstock ; basal leaves oblanceolate, 5 to 10 cm long ; flowering stem erect, 1 to 2 dm long, and the pistillate heads larger than those of the male plant. In stony or turfy alpine situations.

Showy everlasting, *Antennaria pulcherrima* (Hook.) Greene, is somewhat similar but taller ; the oblanceolate basal leaves are long-petioled, the blade up to 10 mm broad, prominently three-ribbed, and densely grey-silvery, tomentose ; the female plant may be up to 5 dm tall, the male lower and less common. Often in large clumps on alpine herbmat slopes.

In the somewhat smaller *Antennaria anaphaloides* Rydb. the leaves and stems are slenderer, and the flowering heads much smaller.

Fig. 229    × 2/3

*Antennaria media* Greene
Fig. 230

Matted, from a creeping, leafy, somewhat woody branching base;
the flowering stems usually less than 2 dm tall. Only the female
plant is known. Forming small clumps in rather moist or stony
alpine situations.

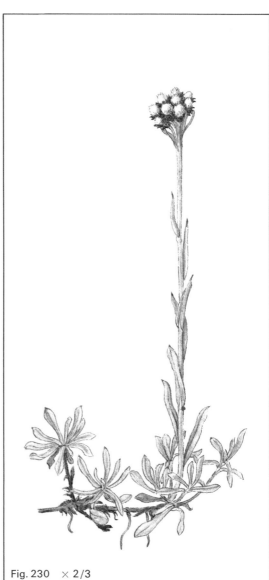

Fig. 230   × 2/3

*Antennaria racemosa* Hook.
**Bunch-flowered Everlasting**
Fig. 231

Plant fresh green with slender, leafy stolons from a stout ascending rootstock, basal leaves oblanceolate, 5 to 6 cm long, tapered to a slender petiole ; flowering stem of the female plant 2 to 4 dm tall, smooth or thinly hairy, that of the male plant lower ; inflorescence elongate of few to several long-peduncled, solitary heads. Openings in subalpine coniferous forest.

Fig. 231    × 3/4

*Antennaria rosea* (D.C. Eat.) Greene
**Pink Everlasting**
Fig. 232

Of matted habit, with freely branching, somewhat woody runners rooting from the nodes, from which rise clusters of leafy flowering stems rarely over 2 dm tall ; flowering heads nodding when young, involucral bracts usually pink. The male plant not known. A rather handsome species, not uncommon in well-drained grassy places at or above timberline.

Fig. 232   × 1/1

*Arnica*
**Arnica**

Perennial herbs with horizontal or ascending rootstocks; opposite, simple, entire or toothed leaves, and showy, mostly radiate, bright yellow heads. Achenes slender, prominently nerved, with a stalkless pappus of hair-like, barbellate, white or brown bristles.

A large genus, in the Canadian Rocky Mountains represented by nearly a score of species, of which a dozen or more are found near or above timberline.

*Arnica cordifolia* Hook.
**Heart-leaved Arnica**
Fig. 233

Stems 3 to 6 dm tall, pubescent, usually with two pairs of rather thin leaves and one very large head or, more often, one terminal large head and two smaller lateral ones from the axils of the uppermost pair of stem-leaves. Common in open coniferous woods and occasionally ascending to timberline.

Fig. 233 × 1/2

*Arnica mollis* Hook.
Fig. 234

Stems often 6 dm tall, slender, glandular-pubescent; leaves three or four pairs, lanceolate, the upper stalkless; head large and solitary or sometimes also with a pair of smaller, lateral heads; achenes hirsute and the pappus pale reddish-brown. Common, usually in damp, grassy places, ascending to or slightly above timberline.

*Arnica lonchophylla* Greene
Fig. 235

Stems mostly solitary, up to 4 dm tall, glandular-puberulent, commonly with three pairs of narrowly lanceolate leaves, the lowermost tapering into a narrow petiole. Heads solitary or with one or two smaller heads from the axils of the uppermost stem-leaves. Pappus white.

*Arnica alpina* (L.) Olin is similar to *A.lonchophylla*, but leaves are all sessile, the upper linear-lanceolate. The head is solitary, or tall specimens often also have two smaller and lateral heads in the axils of the uppermost stem-leaves.

The achenes are hirsute with a white pappus. North America; arctic-alpine.

In the ssp. *tomentosa* the stems are lower and densely tomentose below the single head.

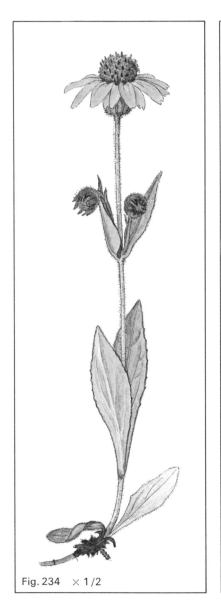

Fig. 234  × 1/2

Fig. 235  × 1/2

*Arnica louiseana* Farr ssp. *frigida* (C.A. Mey.) Maguire
**Lake Louise Arnica**
Fig. 236

Dwarf species, usually with several stems and clusters of basal leaves from a scaly, branching rootstock ; leaves all basal, oblanceolate, and coarsely serrate ; the solitary pale yellow head from a naked peduncle. In moist places, often by alpine brooks.

Fig. 236   × 5/4

*Artemisia*
**Wormwood**

A large, taxonomically difficult genus of perennial and mostly strongly aromatic, grey- or silvery-pubescent herbs or dwarf shrubs with alternate, usually once- or twice-pinnately divided leaves and small discoid heads in a panicled or spike-like inflorescence, commonly nodding when young; the marginal flowers, when present, without a ligule; disk flowers perfect and fertile, and the achenes smooth and without a pappus.

In Alberta represented by about a dozen species, most of which inhabit dry prairies or foothills.

*Artemisia Michauxiana* Bess.
**Michaux's Wormwood**
Fig. 237

Stems leafy, 2 to 4 dm tall, and usually several from a branching, somewhat woody base; leaves 3 to 5 cm long and bipinnately divided, the sections linear, tomentose beneath and green above; heads numerous in an elongated, spike-like raceme. Rocky Mountains.

Northern wormwood (*Artemisia borealis* Pall.) has several 2-to-4-dm-tall stems from a thick, branched taproot; leaves mainly basal and clustered, grey-green from dense and silky pubescence, the blade once or twice pinnate; heads small and numerous, in an elongate and narrow panicle. Stony or gravelly places in the mountains. Circumpolar, arctic-alpine.

Pasture wormwood (*Artemisia frigida* Willd.) is an aromatic, prostrate dwarf shrub, often forming large, dense mats; leaves very small, silvery white, and densely clustered on the branches. Common locally on dry foothill slopes.

Fig. 237   × 3/4

*Aster*
**Aster**

Perennial, late summer- or autumn-flowering herbs with alternate, entire, or toothed leaves, and with solitary but more often several showy and radiate heads; the involucral bracts more or less over-lapping in two or more series; the receptacle naked and usually convex; rayflowers female and fertile, blue, violet, or white; the disk flowers also perfect and fertile, red, yellow, or white; achenes with a pappus of hair-like bristles.

A large, taxonomically difficult genus, not very clearly differentiated from the genus *Erigeron* (flea-bane); in the parks represented by a couple of dozen species, mainly in the foothills and lowland. The following are among the few that are commonly met with above timberline.

*Aster laevis* L. var. *Geyeri* A. Gray
**Smooth Aster**
Fig. 238

Smooth and blue-green, with one to several rather stout, 3-to-8-dm-tall, leafy stems; the lower leaves with a broad-winged leaf-stalk, the upper smaller and stalkless, all minutely serrate in the margins. Heads mostly several in an open showy panicle; the rays blue or light purple. North America; alpine.

In *Aster alpinus* L. ssp. *Vierhapperi* Onno, the stems are mostly solitary and rather stout, commonly less than 3 dm tall, pubescent or woolly, from a stout, leafy base. Lower leaves oblanceolate with blunt or rounded tips, upper ones linear. Heads solitary with pale purplish or nearly white rays. Common on dry grassy slopes, occasionally ascending to timberline.

Fig. 238   × 1/2

*Aster sibiricus* L.
Fig. 239

Stems ascending, 1 to 4 dm tall, simple or branching and commonly clustered from a slender, creeping rootstock ; the leaves oblanceolate, 5 to 7 cm long, smooth above, deep green and somewhat hairy beneath, with entire or serrated margins. Heads one to several, with purplish or blue rays. Siberia and northwestern America.

Fig. 239  × 4/5

*Chrysopsis villosa* Nutt.
**Golden Aster**
Fig. 240

Tufted, greyish green perennial herb, usually with several ascending, 2-to-3-dm-tall stems bearing numerous oblanceolate, stalkless leaves and three or sometimes more flowering heads. Common mainly in the foothills, on dry, sunny slopes, where it often forms large clumps, but only occasionally ascending to near timberline. Cordilleran.

Fig. 240 ×1/1

*Crepis nana* Richards.
**Dwarf Hawksbeard**
Fig. 241

Dwarf perennial with a small, flat rosette of somewhat fleshy, smooth, blue-green leaves, and usually numerous small, yellow heads, borne on short peduncles and barely elevated above the leafy rosette. By its slender and branching rootstock it is well adapted to sliderock habitats in the high-alpine zone. Asia and North America ; arctic-alpine.

At lower elevations and in the foothills, the taller Cordilleran *Crepis elegans* Hook. often forms dense clumps with numerous erect flowering stems up to 2 to 3 dm tall, terminating in a panicle of small, yellow-flowered heads.

Fig. 241 × 1/1

## *Erigeron*
## Flea-Bane

Large, taxonomically difficult genus, closely related to the genus *Aster*. Flowering heads radiate, solitary or few, borne on naked peduncles ; ligules of rayflowers white or, less often, lilac or yellow. The basal leaves alternate, often hairy, their margins entire, or in some species toothed or even finely dissected. In the Canadian Rocky Mountains represented by about two dozen species, of which more than half are alpine and always perennial.

### *Erigeron aureus* Greene
### Golden Flea-Bane
Fig. 242

Dwarf species with a freely branched rootstock, each branch terminating in a small rosette of oval, deep green, petiolate, entire or finely toothed leaves. It is common locally on turfy high-alpine slopes, where it is easily spotted by its relatively large, bright golden-yellow heads.

In similar situations but at lower elevation, occurs the much larger tufted flea-bane (*Erigeron caespitosus* Nutt.), which, in addition to being larger, has stout, ascending, tufted stems from a branched base. Leaves crowded, oblanceolate, with a narrow petiole, and like the stem, grey-green from a dense, short pubescence. The heads solitary or few together, with pale pink or white rays.

### *Erigeron compositus* Pursh
### Compound-leaved Flea-Bane
Fig. 243

Stems 10 to 15 cm tall, one from each division of an often branched base. Basal leaves numerous, ternately or bi-ternately divided and more or less glandular ; the more common var. *glabratus* Macoun with white or lilac rays, and the somewhat smaller and less common var. *discoideus* A. Gray without rayflowers. Both inhabit alpine and gravelly slopes or rocky ledges, ascending at least to 8,700 ft.

Also high alpine is the rare somewhat smaller flea-bane, *Erigeron pallens* Cronq., which forms loose cushions from a slender branching base ; the numerous oblanceolate, entire or three-lobed leaves soft-hairy ; flowering heads solitary, on slender peduncles ; involucral bracts with soft, sticky hairs, and the rayflowers white or pink.

Fig. 242 × 4/5

Fig. 243 × 1/1

*Erigeron grandiflorus* Hook.
**Large-flowered Flea-Bane**
Fig. 244

Stems simple, 10 to 15 cm tall from a decumbent base; leaves mainly basal, oblanceolate, entire, and conspicuously ciliate, those of the stems much smaller and linear. Heads solitary and very showy, 3 to 4 cm in diameter; the involucral bracts villous, with peculiar, flattened, and conspicuously multicellular hairs; rayflowers pale blue, linear, and very numerous; the pappus in double rows. High-alpine rocky slopes and ledges.

Fig. 244 × 5/4

*Erigeron lanatus* Hook.
**Hairy Flea-Bane**
Fig. 245

Stems solitary or several, scapose, and rarely over 25 cm tall,
from a slender branching rootstock, well adapted to an unstable
sloping, gravelly habitat. Leaves in a basal rosette, oblanceolate,
commonly three-toothed, and like the scape densely hoary from a
loose, woolly pubescence. Heads large, up to 3 cm in diameter
when fully expanded, the involucre very prominent and also very
woolly from white or purplish, crinkly, and cross-walled hairs. The
very numerous rayflowers white or pale lilac. High alpine and often
on shale sliderock.

*Erigeron radicatus* Hook. is rather similar
but rarely more than 10 cm tall, with
glabrous or finely pubescent, entire-
leaved rosettes, and white rayflowers.

In similar situations as *Erigeron lanatus*,
but in Canada thus far known only from
a single collection in the eastern foothill
ranges.

*Erigeron peregrinus* (Pursh) Greene
Fig. 246

Stems leafy, mostly simple and up to 7 dm tall, glabrous or villous
below the head. Basal leaves oblanceolate and petiolate, those of the
stem stalkless and much smaller. Heads large and very showy, up to
5 cm in diameter, and commonly solitary, with lilac or pale pink or
white rayflowers. Often in dense clumps by alpine rivulets or in damp
alpine meadows. In the Rocky Mountain parks represented by the
inland race ssp. *callianthemus* (Greene) Cronq., which differs by
having glandular involucral bracts and reduced upper cauline leaves.

Fig. 245 × 2/3

Fig. 246 × 3/4

*Gaillardia aristata* Pursh
**Brown-eyed Susan**
Fig. 247

Perennial herb with a slender, branching rootstock; stems leafy,
up to 6 dm tall, simple or branching; the leaves alternate,
oblanceolate, the lower petioled, entire or toothed or sometimes
pinnately divided. The flowering heads long-peduncled, solitary, large,
and very showy, up to 6 cm in diameter. Often in small clumps on
sunny and well-drained slopes, mainly in the foothills.

*Haplopappus Lyallii* A. Gray
Fig. 248

Dwarf herbaceous perennial from a branching, sub-woody rootstock;
stems rarely more than 10 cm high and densely covered by oblanceolate, entire-margined, glabrous, sessile leaves, terminating in a
single head of deep-yellow flowers; the achenes smooth or sparsely
hirsute with a pappus of white, hair-like bristles. Forming small clumps
or colonies on shaly alpine slopes, in Banff Park ascending to 8,700 feet.

*Haplopappus uniflorus* (Hook.) Torrey &
Gray has one or more ascending, leafy,
2-to-3-dm-tall stems, each with a single
head; the stem- and basal-leaves lanceolate, usually sharply dentate. Sandy
river terraces, mainly in the foothills, but
in the parks known only from the upper
Saskatchewan River.

Fig. 247 × 2/3

Fig. 248 × 1/1

*Hieracium*
**Hawkweed**

Perennial and mostly somewhat glandular-hairy herbs with alternate and mostly basal, entire- or dentate-margined leaves from a stout ascending base. Flowering heads few to many in an open panicle ; the flowers all ligulate, yellow, orange, or white. The achenes tapering at both ends and ribbed, with a pappus of white or yellowish bristles.

A large, taxonomically difficult genus, represented in the Alberta mountains by half a dozen species.

*Hieracium gracile* Hook.
**Slender Hawkweed**
Fig. 249

Flowering stems slender, up to 3 dm tall, scapose or with one or more reduced and sessile leaves, glandular and black-hirsute, especially in the upper part. The inflorescence elongated, of three or more small heads, their involucre glandular-hairy, and the flower yellow ; pappus bristles white. Alpine herbmats.

White hawkweed (*Hieracium albiflorum* Hook.) is tufted, with flowering stems up to 8 dm tall, leafy and yellowish-hirsute below, naked and nearly glabrous above, with oblong, up to 4-cm-broad, long-pubescent leaves, the blade narrowing to a winged petiole. Flowers white or cream-coloured. Dry grassy slopes or river terraces.

*Hieracium Scouleri* Hook. is rather similar, but flowers are yellow, and the involucre is glandular under a dense cover of long, white hairs. Moist alpine woods.

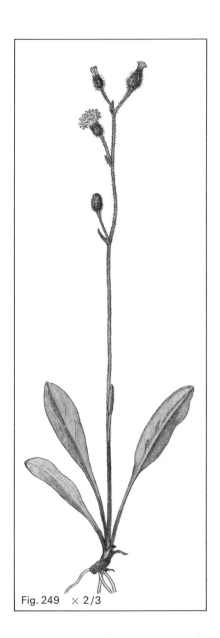

Fig. 249 × 2/3

*Petasites hyperboreus* Rydb.
**Sweet Coltsfoot**
Fig. 250

Stout perennial herb with a horizontally creeping, somewhat fleshy rootstock and mainly basal, long-petioled leaves with a broadly triangular or heart-shaped, irregularly and sinuately lobed blade, deep green, glabrous above and somewhat tomentose beneath. The 3-to-4-dm-tall flowering scapes scaly and appearing early in spring before the leaves. Heads few to several in an elongating flat-topped cluster, each with numerous small, white or pinkish flowers. Damp alpine meadows or in wet moss by alpine brooks.

Arrow-leaved coltsfoot, *Petasites sagittatus* (Pursh) Gray, differs by its arrow-shaped, sinuate-dentate or, at most, shallowly lobed leaf-blades. It grows in boggy places but does not ascend to timberline.

Fig. 250   × 2/3

*Saussurea densa* (Hook.) Rydb.
Fig. 251

Stems mostly solitary, 1 to 2 dm tall, from a short ascending rootstock; leaves very numerous, mainly cauline, their margins sinuate-dentate, conspicuously cobwebby-hirsute beneath. Heads all discoid, crowded; the flowers bright purple; pappus double, the outer of short, rigid bristles, the inner feathery. Not uncommon in moist alpine tundra. The only member of the genus in the area.

Fig. 251   × 1/1

*Senecio*
**Groundsel or Ragwort**

A large, taxonomically complex genus of mostly perennial herbs with alternate, entire or variously toothed or lobed leaves, and one solitary or, more often, several to numerous radiate heads with yellow or orange rays, and five- to ten-ribbed achenes with a pappus of soft, white bristles. In the area the genus is represented by a score or so of native species, of which less than half are alpine.

*Senecio canus* Hook.
**Prairie Groundsel**
Fig. 252

Tufted, from a stout ascending rootstock. Stems simple, solitary or several, up to 4 dm tall; basal leaves oblanceolate, petioled, grey-green or densely tomentose, especially beneath; leaves of the flowering stem smaller with toothed margins. Heads several and large in an open umbel; involucral bract uniformly green and the rays bright yellow. Turfy places in the foothills and in open subalpine forest.

*Senecio lugens* Richards. is similar but glabrous, or at most sparsely woolly and blue-green. At once distinguished from *Senecio canus* by its black-tipped involucral bracts. Common in rather wet alpine tundra. These black-tipped bracts suggested the specific name (from the Latin word *lugeo*, meaning "to mourn") to Sir John Richardson, who was the first to collect this plant, near Bloody Falls on the Coppermine River. The allusion is to the massacre there of a band of unsuspecting Eskimos by the Indian warriors who in 1771 accompanied Samuel Hearne on his expedition to the Arctic Coast.

*Senecio Freemontii* T. & G.
Fig. 253

Glabrous and somewhat fleshy dwarf species, often of matted habit, from a branching and ascending base; stems freely branching, often wine-red, with scattered, obovate or spatulate, and toothed leaves; heads solitary and relatively large, at the end of the branches. Moist mossy or gravelly places by cold alpine steams. Cordilleran.

Fig. 252 × 1/2

Fig. 253 × 4/5

*Senecio pauciflorus* Pursh
Fig. 254

Essentially glabrous, with simple stems up to 5 dm tall from a stout, ascending rootstalk; leaves dark green, somewhat fleshy, the basal ones long-petioled with an elliptic blade, those of the stem pinnatifid and sessile. Heads several, mostly discoid but sometimes radiate; the disk flowers bright red, the rayflowers yellow. Common in moist alpine meadows.

*Senecio pauperculus* Michx. is lower, and the stems are slender and glabrous, at least in age, except for tufts of white matted hairs in the leaf-axils; basal leaves clustered, slender-petioled, the oblong blade entire or serrate, those of the stem often pinnate and smaller. Heads several on slender peduncles, the rayflowers dark yellow. Subalpine tundra. Both North America.

*Senecio resedifolius* Less. is a high-alpine dwarf species, rarely over 10 cm tall; the basal leaves are petiolate, blade somewhat fleshy, ovate or kidney-shaped, entire or more often toothed; heads commonly solitary, discoid or radiate, with purplish involucral bracts and yellow or reddish flowers. Amphi-Beringian.

*Senecio triangularis* Hook.
Fig. 255

Essentially glabrous, with very leafy stems up to 1.5 m tall, from a stout rootstock; the heads few to many in a flat-topped raceme; leaves fresh green, petiolate, the lower triangular, the upper lanceolate, their margins coarsely toothed. Moist places by alpine streams or in meadows, often in large clumps or colonies. Cordilleran.

Fig. 254 × 2/3

Fig. 255 × 2/3

*Solidago multiradiata* Ait. ssp. *scopulorum* Gray
**Rocky Mountain Goldenrod**
Fig. 256

Stems 2 to 3 dm tall, leafy, in clusters from a sub-woody branching base. Perhaps the commonest and showiest of the dozen or so goldenrods native to the parks. It is common on dry open slopes or in open willow-thickets, on river flats and on terraces, but rarely ascends beyond timberline.

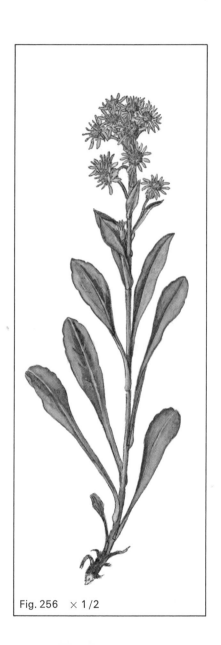

Fig. 256   × 1/2

*Taraxacum*
**Dandelion**

Stemless perennials with milky juice, from a fleshy taproot; leaves
in a basal rosette, oblong, coarsely toothed, the teeth mostly down-
ward directed, rarely entire; heads solitary on a slender, tubular scape;
involucral bracts in two or three series, the outer shorter than the inner,
in some species reflexed in age; flowers strap-like, mainly yellow;
achenes spindle-shaped, strongly ribbed and spiny, with a slender
beak several times longer than the body and terminating in an
umbrella-shaped pappus of hair-like bristles.

Most of the dandelions seen in the parks are the common introduced
roadside weeds; the few native species are comparatively rare, and
mainly alpine.

*Taraxacum scopulorum* Rydb.
**Rocky Mountain Dandelion**
Fig. 257

Diminutive, glabrous plant, with a small rosette of toothed leaves
less than 10 cm long and commonly longer than the more or less
decumbent, reddish scapes; the heads are small and barely expanded
at flowering time. High alpine.

In *Taraxacum ovinum* Greene the leaves
are entire-margined or at most have
short but sharp teeth, and the scape is
tomentose below the head, which is
normally expanded during anthesis.
High alpine.

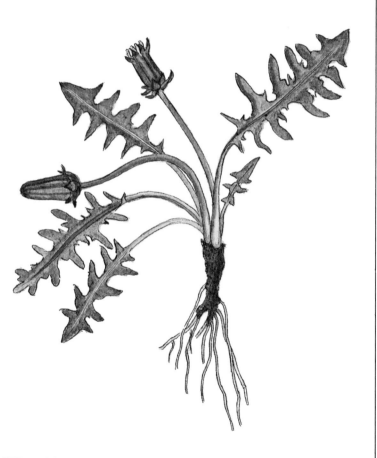

Fig. 257  × 5/4

*Townsendia Parryi* D.C. Eat.
Fig. 258

Biennial. A rosette of deep-green, oblanceolate leaves are formed
the first year, followed the year after by one or several flowering
stems, each terminating in a very showy radiate head up to 5 or 6 cm
in diameter ; the central disk-flowers are deep yellow, and the
rayflowers have broad, purplish blue ligules. Dry grassy slopes
mainly in the foothills.

More common but much less showy is
the perennial *Townsendia exscapa*
(Richards.) Porter, with numerous narrowly lanceolate leaves and small,
sessile, yellow-flowering heads, partly
hidden among the leaves.

Fig. 258 × 1/1

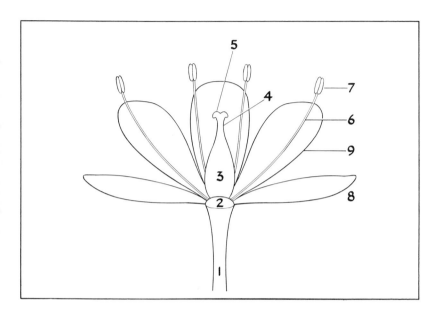

Schematic diagram of a perfect, or bisexual flower, in which the petals and sepals are free, that is, not united.

**1** Pedicel, or peduncle (stalk of flower)

**2** Receptacle (part of flower that supports sepals, petals, stamens, and pistil, that is, female parts of flower)

| | |
|---|---|
| **3** Ovary | |
| **4** Style | Pistil |
| **5** Stigma | |
| **6** Filament (stalk of anther) | Stamen (male parts of flower) |
| **7** Anther | |
| **8** Sepal (segment of calyx) | |
| **9** Petal (segment of corolla) | |

# Botanical Vocabulary

**Achene**
A small, nut-like fruit, as in the separate fruits of a buttercup

**Alternate**
Not opposite, singly at each node

**Ament**
A catkin or a dry, scaly spike, such as the inflorescence of willow

**Annual**
Of one year's duration

**Anther**
The pollen-bearing part of a stamen

**Anthesis**
Period during which a flower is fully expanded or functional

**Appressed**
Lying close or flat against a surface

**Ascending**
Rising obliquely

**Awn**
A bristle-shaped appendage

**Axil**
The angle between leaf and stem

**Axillary**
Growing in an axil

**Axis (pl. axes)**
The central or longitudinal support of organs such as flowers in an inflorescence

**Barbellate**
With short, stiff hairs and bristles

**Biennial**
Of two years' duration

**Bisexual**
With both stamens and pistils

**Bract**
A modified leaf borne on a floral axis

**Bulbiferous**
Bearing bulbs

**Bulbil**
A small, usually bulb-like body produced in a leaf-axis, or replacing the flowers

**Caespitose**
Matted or tufted

**Calcareous**
Of soil rich in lime

**Calyx**
The outermost floral bracts or members, usually green

**Cannescent**
Hoary with grey pubescence

**Capitate**
Head-shaped, or forming a dense cluster

**Capsule**
A dry fruit composed of several carpels opening by valves

**Carpel**
A simple pistil, or a member of a compound pistil

**Catkin**
An ament, or a dry, scaly, spike-like inflorescence, as in willow

**Cauline**
Belonging to the stem

**Chaffy**
Covered with scales

**Ciliate**
Fringed with hairs

**Corm**
Bulb-like, enlarged base of stem

**Corolla**
The petals of a flower, collectively

**Corymb**
Round or flat-topped type of inflorescence in which the axis is short and the lower pedicels relatively long

**Crenate**
Dentate with distinctly rounded teeth

**Crenulate**
Minutely crenate

**Cryptogams**
Plants lacking true flowers and fruits, such as ferns and mosses

**Culm**
The stem of grasses or sedges

**Cyme**
A terminal, usually broad and flattened inflorescence in which the central flowers are the first to open

**Deciduous**
Not persistent, soon falling

**Decumbent**
Lying flat on the ground, but with ascending tips

**Dentate**
Toothed

**Depressed**
Flattened, diffuse, loosely spreading

**Dioecious**
Unisexual, with male and female flowers appearing on separate plants or in separate parts of the inflorescence

**Discoid**
Disk-like; in the Composite Family, of a head without rayflowers

**Disk flowers**
In the Composite Family, the tubular flowers in a head

**Dorsal**
Belonging to the back of an organ

**Drupe**
A fleshy or pulpy, one- to several-seeded fruit, such as a cherry

**Emergent**
Of water plants only partly submersed

**Endemic**
Confined geographically to a limited area

**Entire**
Without indentations or division

**Erect**
Growing essentially in an erect position

**Evergreen**
Remaining green throughout the winter

**Exserted**
Projecting beyond; often referring to stamens or styles from a corolla

**Filament**
The stalk of a stamen bearing the anther

**Filiform**
Thread-shaped

**Floret**
A small flower, usually one of several in a cluster

**Frond**
The leaf-like part of a fern or fern-like plant

**Fruit**
The seed-bearing part of a plant

**Glabrous**
Smooth and without hairs

**Glaucous**
Covered or whitened by a bloom, as in the skin of a grape

**Globose**
Having the shape of a globe or a sphere

**Glume**
A chaff-like bract; in grasses one of the two empty bracts at the base of the spikelet

**Habit**
The general appearance of a plant

**Habitat**
The kind of place in which a plant grows, such as bogs, woods, etc.

**Herb**
A plant dying back to the ground at the end of the growing season

**Herbmat**
Matted alpine or arctic plant community, composed mainly of low, herbaceous plants

**Hirsute**
Pubescent with rather coarse or stiff hairs

**Inflorescence**
The flowering cluster of a plant

**Internode**
The part of a stem between two nodes

**Involucre**
The row of bracts surrounding a single flower, a cluster of flowers, or a head

**Irregular**
Of a flower composed of parts dissimilar in form or size

**Keel**
The two lowermost and united petals of the butterfly-shaped flowers peculiar to members of the Pea Family

**Lanceolate**
Shaped like the head of a lance, broadest near the base, narrowing toward the apex

**Lax**
Not dense, usually of an inflorescence

**Legume**
The fruit of members of the Pea Family

**Lemma**
The lower of the two bracts enclosing the individual grass-flower

**Ligule**
The strap- or tongue-like limb of the marginal flower in the Composite Family; the flat, usually membranaceous projection from the summit of the sheath in grasses

**Linear**
Narrow and parallel-margined

**Lobe**
A segment of an organ, especially if rounded

**Locule**
The cavity of an ovary or an anther

**Membranaceous**
Thin and more or less translucent

**Midrib**
The median or central rib of a leaf

**Monoecious**
With stamens and pistils in separate flowers, but in the same plant

**Naked**
Lacking various organs or appendages, especially when such are usually present in similar species or parts

**Nerve**
An unbranched vein or slender rib

**Node**
The solid constriction in the culm of a grass; places on a stem where a leaf or a whorl of leaves is attached

**Oblanceolate**
Lanceolate with the broadest part above the middle

**Obovate**
Ovate with the narrower end basal, as in a leaf

**Obovoid**
Egg-shaped, with the broad end toward the apex

**Obtuse**
Blunt

**Offset**
A short, prostrate or ascending shoot, usually propagative in function, arising near the base of the plant

**Opposite**
Situated diametrically opposite each other at the same node

**Ovoid**
Egg-shaped

**Palea or Palet**
The tiny, upper bract that, with the lemma, encloses the flower

**Palmate**
Diverging radiately like fingers or lobes

**Panicle**
A compound or branched inflorescence of the racemose type

**Pappus**
The tufts of hairs on the achene of many species of the Composite Family

**Pedicel**
The stem or support of a single flower

**Peduncle**
A primary flower-stalk supporting either a cluster or a solitary flower

**Perennial**
Of several or many years' duration

**Perfect**
Of a flower having both stamens and pistils

**Perigynium**
The inflated sac enclosing the ovary in *Carex*

**Persistent**
Long-continuous, such as the calyx of some fruits, or of leaves lasting through the winter

**Petal**
A division of the corolla

**Petiole**
Leaf-stalk

**Pilose**
Hairy with short, soft hairs

**Pinna (pl. pinnae)**
One of the primary divisions of a pinnate or compoundly pinnate leaf

**Pinnate**
Of a compound leaf in which the leaflets appear on each side of the common axis; hence, pinnatifid, pinnately cleft

**Pistil**
The seed-bearing organ of a flower, consisting of ovary, stigma, and (when present) style

**Pistillate**
Usually of flowers containing only the female parts

**Plumose**
Feathery

**Pod**
A one- or two-locular fruit, some opening by two valves falling away from the frame on which the seeds develop, and across which a membranaceous partition is formed, or splitting along one side only (follicle)

**Pollen**
The fertilizing, powder-like substance produced by the anthers of a flower

**Prostrate**
Lying flat on the ground

**Puberulent**
Minutely pubescent

**Pubescence**
Hair cover, without reference to structure

**Pubescent**
Hairy, especially with short, soft hairs

**Raceme**
A simple inflorescence of pedicellate flowers on a common, more or less elongated axis, the lowermost flowers opening first

**Rachis**
The axis of an inflorescence or of a compound leaf

**Radiate**
Spreading from a common centre ; in the inflorescence of the Composite Family

**Rayflower**
The ligulate or strap-like marginal flower in the Composite Family

**Receptacle**
The expanded part of an axis bearing the organs of a flower

**Reticulate**
Net-veined

**Revolute**
Rolled backward from the margins

**Rhizome**
A horizontal or ascending underground stem rooting at the nodes

**Rib**
A primary and prominent vein of a leaf

**Rootstock, equals Rhizome**

**Rosette**
A circular cluster of leaves

**Saccate**
Formed like a bag or a pouch

**Scale**
A thin, often translucent bract or body, usually a degenerate leaf

**Scape**
A naked flowering stem rising directly from the ground

**Scapose**
Bearing or resembling a scape

**Scree, equals Talus**

**Scurfy**
Covered with scale-like protuberances

**Seed**
The ripened ovule, consisting of the ripened embryo and its several coats

**Sepal**
A division of the calyx

**Serrate**
Having sharp, forward-pointing teeth

**Serrulate**
Finely serrate

**Sessile**
Without a stalk

**Sheath**
A tubular envelope, such as the lower part of the leaf in grasses

**Silique, equals Pod**

**Simple**
Not divided, entire

**Sinuate**
Wavy, especially of leaf margins

**Snowbed**
Place where, owing to topographical
features of the landscape, a thick layer of
snow accumulates each winter

**Sorus (pl. sori)**
Term applied to the fruit-dots of the fern

**Spatulate**
Flat and oblong, downward-narrowed,
like a druggist's spatula

**Sphagnum**
Peat moss

**Spicate**
Arranged in spikes

**Spike**
An inflorescence with sessile flowers
along a common elongated axis

**Spikelet**
A small or secondary spike subtended
by a common pair of glumes or bracts,
as in grasses

**Spinulose**
Covered by tiny spines

**Spore**
The reproductive organ in cryptogams
corresponding to the seed in flowering
plants, but containing no embryo

**Spur**
The hollow, sac-like or tubular exten-
sion from the base of a petal in certain
flowers

**Stamen**
The pollen-bearing organ of a flower,
consisting of filament and anther

**Standard**
The uppermost petal of a flower in the
Pea Family

**Stellate**
Of sessile or short-stalked, star-shaped
hairs

**Stem**
The main ascending axis of a plant, as
contrasted to the root and leaf

**Sterile**
Unproductive

**Stigma**
The part of the pistil that receives the
pollen

**Stipe**
A stalk-like support; the "leaf-stalk" of
a fern; the support of a pistil; hence
stipitate, having a stipe

**Stipule**
Appendage at the base of the petiole;
hence stipulate, with stipules

**Stolon**
A horizontally spreading branch or
runner usually rooting at the nodes

**Stoloniferous**
Producing stolons

**Strigose**
Covered with small, straight,
appressed, hair-like scales

**Strobile**
A cone-like inflorescence

**Style**
The attenuated part of a pistil connecting
the stigma to the ovary

**Submersed**
Growing or adapted to grow under
water

**Subulate**
Awl-shaped

**Talus**
Rocky debris at the foot of a rock wall

**Taproot**
A primary descending root

**Taxonomy**
Classification

**Ternate**
Arranged in threes

**Tomentose**
Densely pubescent with matted wool

**Tuber**
A rootless, thickened, short underground
organ serving for food storage and also
for propagation, e.g. potato

**Umbel**
An inflorescence in which the pedicels
spring from the same central level

**Unarmed**
Lacking thorns or spines

**Unisexual**
Of flowers bearing stamens or pistils,
but not both

**Valve**
One of the parts into which a capsule
splits when ripe

**Vascular**
Of plants having vessels or ducts

**Villous or Villose**
Hairy, with long, soft, but not matted
hairs

**Viscid**
Glutinous, sticky

**Viviparous**
Of vegetative buds sprouting or germi-
nating on the parent plant

**Whorl**
Such as in leaves arranged in a circle
around the stem

**Wing**
A flat structure emerging from the side
of an organ ; in the Pea Family the
lateral and similar petals

**Winter bud**
A shortened, crowded, hibernating
vegetative shoot

# Index